Time to Write

43 Standards-based Lessons for Developing Creative Writing

R. E. Myers

A GOOD YEAR BOOK™

Good Year Books
Tucson, Arizona

Dedication

To my son Ted, with the greatest admiration and affection.

Good Year Books

Are available for most basic curriculum subjects plus many enrichment areas. For more Good Year Books, contact your local bookseller or educational dealer. For a complete catalog with information about other Good Year Books, please contact:

Good Year Books
P.O. Box 91858
Tucson, AZ 85752-1858
www.goodyearbooks.com

Cover design and photo: Gary D. Smith, Performance Design
Text design: Doug Goewey
Drawings: Sean O'Neill

Preface

*T*ime to Write is not a short course in how to become a professional writer. Nor is it a "by-the-numbers" course in composition. What this book targets is broader and more vague: a student's growth in self-expression. To be truthful, there is an infinite number of ways in which teachers can encourage students to express themselves in words. It is not really difficult to think of devices for stimulating young people to write. However, it *is* difficult to work with each student in such a way that his or her abilities to think and to express himself or herself will grow. Most of the time teachers hope that students will acquire skills and insights as a result of an exposure to literature, life, and teachers' attempts to analyze and clarify issues of grammar, punctuation, spelling, and style. It is a hit-or-miss procedure, but there is none better.

This book does not purport to solve the English teacher's eternal dilemma, but it does attempt to shift some of the responsibility for growth back to where it belongs—on the student's shoulders. Thus I have included self-evaluation techniques in several of the exercises. By inviting students to judge their stories with a scoring guide, by asking them whether they were successful in devising their own exercise in logical thinking after they have tried it out on someone, and by repeatedly asking them to select their most promising reaction in a stimulus word, I have attempted to persuade students that they are capable of evaluating their progress in writing—with your guidance.

In addition to helping students become more self-critical (in a positive way), I hope to encourage them to become more perceptive in viewing their world. That world includes the here and now, and so I have presented them with rather challenging questions regarding their surroundings. Their world also includes this troubled planet, and so I have asked them to think about relationships among countries and peoples. Most importantly, their world is colored and shaped by their own feelings, and so I have invited them to think about themselves and their reactions to a variety of things. If you present students with these exercises at judicious moments, the results could be highly beneficial.

Time to Write, like nearly all of the titles of its units, has several meanings. First of all, it means students should have enough time in which to react to ideas, to digest them, and then to formulate their own ideas in a manner that is consistent with their values and skills. Second, it means that it is high time that students learn to write; when they have reached middle school, we believe they should have begun to develop the skills of expression that will mean so much to them personally and professionally. Finally, *Time to Write* is a book for a student's private thoughts; it is a receptacle, a storage place, for ideas when he or she feels it is time to write. I sincerely hope that this book can be all of these things to you and your students.

—R. E. Myers

Contents

Contents

Contents

Introduction

Getting Students Ready to Write

To obtain satisfactory writing efforts from your students, you should create an atmosphere in which there is no threat of evaluation or ridicule. Although young people are naturally fearful of what their peers may do or say when they attempt to express themselves, you can set an example that will be contagious by being nonjudgmental and accepting.

The warm-up or pre-writing stage is particularly important. You must ready students for their thinking and writing by leading into the lessons with appropriate remarks and activities. For example, you can talk about funny misconceptions, show objects or pictures, project transparencies, or play recordings in order to get boys and girls into a writing mood. Note that oral warm-ups are most effective.

Be careful, though, not to put thoughts into their heads. Let their writing result from their own perceptions and insights, not yours. If you can pull off this kind of lesson, you will be delighted with the ideas your students will express.

The Writing Process

After students get their ideas down on paper, the next step is to encourage them to *reflect* upon those ideas. Give them time to consider what they have written. Then they can examine the structure of their writing. That is, after writing two or more sentences, they can examine the order in which they have set down their ideas. Then they can determine whether these notions are consistent with one another ("Does it make sense?"). This activity leads naturally into any rewriting that they find necessary. Students as young as eleven are capable of writing several drafts.

When they are satisfied that they are saying what they want to say, your students can attend to the formal aspects of writing, such as spelling, punctuation, grammar, and manuscript form. (Incidentally, most teachers agree that in the early stages of inspiration it is disastrous to insist that they worry about these matters, and it is inappropriate to fret about handwriting—if students are not use word-processing software—until the final draft.) It is terribly important that they do their own proofreading. Otherwise, the mistakes that you point out could block them from developing their own ideas.

The wise writing teacher, however, does engage in a certain amount of "guiding." Without resorting to the red pencil, he or she can ask pertinent questions about both the form and the substance of the student's work. Students do not usually resent a supportive teacher who asks a few questions during a conference over the first draft.

A last and vital phase begins after students have revised, proofread, corrected, and rewritten their work. This phase occurs when you encourage students—not force them—to share their productions. And, unless a student is especially shy or the writing is very personal, sharing isn't a problem. Students can read their writing aloud or publish it in a student publication. Some teachers like to make bulletin boards of successful assignments. The results of a well-planned and relaxed writing lesson are exciting for the teacher and students alike.

An Overview of the Lessons

There is a wide range of difficulty in the lessons in *Time to Write*. "Winning by Losing," for example, is quite challenging, and so is "A Mixed Blessing." On the other hand, "More or Less" and "A-Mazing" are straightforward and don't make the demands upon a student's knowledge and resources that other lessons do.

By reading through a lesson, you will have a fairly good idea of how your students might respond to it. You won't *know*, of course, because any lesson can have its surprises. The materials in this book are especially designed to bring forth unseen consequences, asking students to think in a way that is different than they are used to doing.

Note that the didactic element is played down in nearly all of the lessons. There are definitions given in some of the lessons, but for the most part the methodology consists of trying to get a student's interest, and then involvement, and then having him or her do some writing as a result. There is little emphasis on making sure that the student knows what a preposition, declarative sentence, or stanza is. *Time to Write* is an *ideabook*, not a workbook.

As suggested above, it is an excellent plan to become thoroughly familiar with instructional material before presenting it to students. For example, if you take a few minutes to read "Finish the Story," you can get an idea of how to administer it and how long it might take for the majority of your students to finish it—if, indeed, you think they should complete all of the lessons. There are nine story starters in the lesson, and you may want to give your students the option of doing only some of them, rather than all of them. You can also adapt or modify any or all of the lessons and thereby improve them.

How to Use This Book

The lessons in this ideabook follow a pattern. It is one that is based upon the creative thinking process. There are usually three parts or levels to an exercise:

1 **The First Level**

Many teachers have found that giving students the initiating or first-level activity orally is a good way to warm them up for a writing experience. The warm-up is a well-established and necessary part of the creative thinking process, and it is especially important in allowing young people to orient their thinking and free themselves of inhibitions. This "playing around" stage is critical for anyone who would attempt to engage in a creative endeavor, and putting words together that have been inspired by one's own mental efforts is certainly a creative activity.

These lessons are an attempt to set the stage for creative-thinking-with-words by contriving situations in which young people will be challenged to combine ideas and elements, redefine objects and processes, elaborate upon ideas, predict consequences, explore possibilities, and analyze ideas. Several of the lessons include humorous situations. Along with a playful attitude, a sense of humor is a wonderful lubricant for freeing a flow of original ideas.

2 **The Second Level**

The second stage generally takes the student a little deeper into the subject. There is a slight push to get the student more involved in thinking about the topic at hand.

3 **The Third Level**

It is quite possible that a class or an individual student won't really accept an invitation at the third level to express themselves. There is an overwhelming amount of evidence that suggests that in creative thinking activities it is probably wise not to demand a product. Encourage, but do not insist.

Following Through

Many lessons include additional extension ideas so you can take students even further with a particular type of writing.

The lessons in this ideabook will appeal to some of your students more than others, just as some parts of the curriculum fascinate some young people but bore others. You should, however, discover that students who generally aren't "turned on" by regular assignments come alive when they are presented with a creative thinking activity. One of your rewards for engaging your students in activities such as these is to see someone who has been indifferent suddenly begin to shine brightly.

All of these lessons convey a conviction that learning and thinking are continuous and personal. To engage in creative thinking is to rely primarily upon one's own resources, so it follows that the individual student must have practice in expressing himself or herself in order to become an independent thinker. This ideabook provides a number of opportunities for students of widely varying talents and backgrounds to think for themselves in a classroom setting.

Lesson 1

Really Good

Producing Synonyms

About the Lesson

"Really Good" is a short lesson that will have students thinking about synonyms. Except when in class, they probably don't worry that they are often repetitious in their choice of words, especially adjectives and verbs. This lesson will probably not alter the way they talk, but it may give them a nudge when it comes to writing compositions and stories.

Targeted Learner Outcomes

The student will:

- produce synonyms for twelve words, and

- rephrase two sentences, replacing the overworked words.

1 The lesson begins with a brief discussion of the nuances in the meanings of adjectives. You might very well enlarge upon what we say with a discussion of words that have no exact synonyms and others that have an abundance of them.

2 The first part of this section of the lesson requires your students to come up with synonyms that come readily to mind for such words as *car*, *fast*, and *funny*. (The main meanings for *funny* are *humorous* and *peculiar* in ordinary language, and most likely one or more of your students will point this out.) The second part of this section asks your students to think of synonyms for six more words that are perhaps less easy to call up, although most of your students will not have to resort to a dictionary.

Common synonyms for the first six words are:

1. car = automobile
2. fast = swift
3. funny = humorous
4. sweat = perspiration (perspire)
5. eyeglasses = spectacles
6. flower = blossom, bloom

These are acceptable synonyms for the next six words:

7. enemy = foe
8. dry = arid
9. calm = tranquil, serene, quiet
10. lie (noun) = falsehood
11. tuneful = melodious
12. trite = stale

There are probably many overworked expressions other than "really good" that could be used in a two- or three-sentence paragraph such as the one in this lesson about Bert. At one time the adjective *awesome* was used so frequently, especially by young people, that the vocabularies of Americans seemed to be devoid of other superlatives. If *awesome* is still in vogue with your students, you might ask them for other adjectives to substitute for it in the following paragraph. They may have a little trouble in doing so.

> "Laura's oldest brother's car is the most awesome one I've seen," enthused Rebecca. "Besides being gorgeous, his Corvette is really cool. If you've ever seen it, you probably just about fainted. Not only is it a great color—it's an awesome shade of red—but it goes really fast!"

3 The two sentences presented in the last section of the lesson are loaded with *really* and *good*. (We believe that the young person speaking would have actually said "*real good*," but for the purposes of this lesson we didn't bother about the grammar.) Students are to find substitutes for those two overworked words. This may be difficult for them.

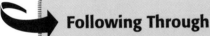

Following Through

Other overworked words such as *you know, totally, hopefully,* and *awesome* could be discussed in conjunction with this lesson. One wonders if we'll ever be free of *you know* in American speech. Words such as *totally* are contagious, and you might also discuss that aspect of language with your students.

Really Good

Name _____ Date _____

1 A synonym is a word that means the same, or nearly the same, as another word. In English, it is difficult to come up with exact synonyms because frequently two synonyms mean something slightly different. For example, *tiny* means something different from *small*, but they both indicate a size that is below average. Nevertheless, we need synonyms to give variety to our speech and writing.

2 Following are words that have interchangeable synonyms. What are the most common synonyms for these words:

1. car _____

2. fast _____

3. funny _____

4. sweat _____

5. eyeglasses _____

6. flower _____

Here are six more words for which there are good synonyms but those words might not come to your mind right away. Try to think of them without referring to a dictionary or thesaurus.

7. enemy _____

8. dry _____

9. calm _____

10. lie (noun) _____

11. tuneful _____

12. trite _____

3 To demonstrate the need for synonyms, here are two sentences that are somewhat boring because of the repetition of two words. Make the two sentences less boring by using some other words in place of *really* and *good*.

> **Bert was a really good singer, and he knew some really good songs. Whenever we were really hurting for entertainment at one of our parties and we wanted to make sure that it would be really good, we asked Bert to sing a song, one that everyone would really like.**

An Even-tempered Coach
Producing Antonyms

About the Lesson

"An Even-tempered Coach" isn't about sports—it's about antonyms. It begins with examples of people saying the opposite of what they mean to say and then asks students to provide antonyms for popular adjectives. It ends with their supplying pairs of adjectives for descriptions of people and things.

Targeted Learner Outcomes

The student will:

- produce antonyms for twelve adjectives, and

- produce pairs of adjectives that contrast the descriptions of subjects.

❶ The first level asks students to produce antonyms for a dozen adjectives. Students should be able to come up with these antonyms easily:

1. full = empty
2. healthy = sickly, unhealthy, ill
3. honest = crooked, dishonest, corrupt
4. soft = hard
5. clean = dirty, unclean
6. brave = cowardly
7. fast = slow
8. difficult = hard, trying
9. expensive = cheap
10. thick = thin, narrow
11. short = tall
12. friendly = hostile, unfriendly

❷ The second part of the lesson presents a more challenging task, that is, finding pairs of adjectives that contrast with ten subjects. These would be acceptable responses, but many others will do as well. If students get stuck, send them to a dictionary or thesaurus.

1. hot-headed and biased coach
2. easy and well-written book
3. secretive, guarded woman
4. young and overfed man
5. corrupt and lazy government official
6. neat and clean room
7. cold, unloving parent
8. benevolent and easy-going businessman
9. expensive and unreliable car
10. virtuous, clear-thinking man

An Even-tempered Coach

Name _____   Date _____

1 Occasionally people say just the opposite of what they mean. Their tongues and their brains aren't quite in sync. At other times they say just the opposite of what they mean in an attempt to be ironic or sarcastic. For example, a person might say "Thanks a lot!" to someone who has just been insulting. On the other hand, antonyms, words that have opposing meanings, are used by writers, not because they want to be ironic, but because they want to compare and contrast two or more things.

Probably the most common of all pairs of antonyms is "good-bad." Others that we use all of the time are *ugly–beautiful, dry–wet, intelligent–stupid, hot–cold,* and *always–never.* What are the most common antonyms for the following adjectives?

1. full _____

2. healthy _____

3. honest _____

4. soft _____

5. clean _____

6. brave _____

7. fast _____

8. difficult _____

9. expensive _____

10. thick _____

11. short _____

12. friendly _____

Where is the best place to find a large number of antonyms? _____

_____

Name _____   Date _____

2 If you wanted to contrast a slick, fast-talking man with someone who has opposing traits, what two adjectives would you use?

_____

What pair of adjectives would you use to compare and contrast these people and things?

1. an even-tempered and fair-minded coach
_____

2. a difficult and poorly written textbook
_____

3. an open, frank woman _____
_____

4. an elderly, wizened man _____
_____

5. an honorable and hard-working government official _____
_____

6. a room that is cluttered and filthy _____

7. a devoted, loving parent _____

8. a mean-spirited and hard-hearted businessman _____
_____

9. an economical and reliable car _____

10. an evil man with a twisted mind _____

Lesson 3
A-mazing
Decoding a Short Message

About the Lesson

This lesson features a simple coded message that is easily broken. Accordingly, both the coded message and the maze won't frustrate most of your students. For those who are not practiced in decoding messages, it will take a bit of time.

Targeted Learner Outcomes

The student will:

- decode a message, and
- solve a maze.

❶ The familiar code in which each letter of the alphabet is represented by the one following it is used in this activity. Thus, TUBSU PGG UP UIF SJHIU translates to "Start off to the right," the clue for getting through the maze quickly.

❷ The maze itself is not terribly difficult, especially if the student solves the coded message and goes to the right instead of the left.

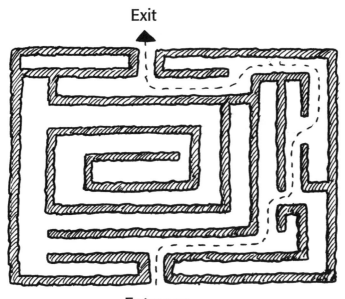

Exit

Entrance

Following Through

Have your students devise their own coded messages and mazes. Encourage them to make up original codes.

Name _____   Date _____

1 Have you ever tried to find your way through a maze? It can be a lot of fun. Below is a sketch of a maze that you can trace your way through with a pencil. But first, solve this simple coded message, which will give you a clue to getting through the maze quickly.

TUBSU PGG UP UIF SJHIU

This is the maze:

Exit

Entrance

2 What was the coded message? _____

What is the key to the code? _____

_____

_____

Lesson 4

The Rhyming Game

Devising a Rhyming Game

About the Lesson

Although this activity is probably familiar to many of your students, many will find it amusing to play with words. Because there is so much rhyming in popular music, students should feel comfortable while responding to the prompts and in making up their own rhymes. The game can also be a vocabulary builder.

Targeted Learner Outcomes

The student will:

- produce twelve pairs of rhyming words that fit the two-word definitions offered, and
- make up six definitions for rhyming pairs of words that have only one syllable each.

1 Remind students that the lesson asks that each of the paired rhyming words have only one syllable. These are acceptable responses to the dozen definitions:

1. torrid child = hot tot
2. large hog = big pig
3. sad friend = glum chum
4. bashful lad = coy boy or shy guy
5. recipe collection = cook book
6. disgusting fashion = bad fad
7. wonderful spouse = great mate
8. unusual twosome = rare pair
9. pleasant fragrance = swell smell
10. superior officer = top cop
11. phony reptile = fake snake
12. dilatory enemy = slow foe

2 You can point out that the twelve rhymed pairs of words each has an adjective preceding a noun. In making up their lists of six hink-pinks, however, it isn't necessary that your students modify the nouns with adjectives. If one of them comes up with something like "bruin's den = bear's lair," it is perfectly all right. (*Bruin's* and *bear's* function as adjectives but are the possessive forms of the nouns.) Have your students check their hink-pinks to see if they have one syllable each.

The Rhyming Game

Name _____ Date _____

1 *Willy-nilly, hanky-panky, mumbo-jumbo, helter-skelter*—there are a number of these rhyming pairs in the English language. There are also *razzle-dazzle, mamby-pamby, hurly-burly, roly-poly, lovey-dovey, hotsy-totsy, hoity-toity,* and *hurdy-gurdy.* A popular game based on rhyming pairs is often called *hink pink* or *hinky-pinky,* depending upon whether the words have one or two syllables. In this game you try to match two rhyming words with two words that mean the same thing.

Let's play the game with only one syllable for each of the paired words. For example, if you see *obese feline,* you can respond with *fat cat.* Try to find rhyming pairs for the words below. If you can't think of a synonym, use a dictionary or thesaurus to find a suitable word.

1. torrid child _____

2. large hog _____

3. sad friend _____

4. bashful lad _____

5. recipe collection _____

6. disgusting fashion _____

7. wonderful spouse _____

8. unusual twosome _____

9. pleasant fragrance _____

10. superior officer _____

11. phony reptile _____

12. dilatory enemy _____

The Rhyming Game (continued)

ACTIVITY

Name _____   Date _____

2 See if you can think of six or more pairs of rhyming words. Write them on the spaces below. Then for each pair give a definition in two or three words on the line below it. Challenge your classmates to come up with rhyming pairs for your definitions.

1. _____

_____

2. _____

_____

3. _____

_____

4. _____

_____

5. _____

_____

6. _____

_____

Lesson 5

Is It Reasonable?

Composing a Limerick

About the Lesson

Young people can be taught the elementary principles of logic. They can learn what inference is, to look for consistency in statements, to understand the terms of a proposition, and to examine the definitions of the terms. They can learn to reason in this way after just a few experiences with activities such as this.

Targeted Learner Outcomes

The student will:

- determine whether seven statements are reasonable or unreasonable,
- devise statements that are reasonable or unreasonable,
- know the form and rhythm of a limerick, and,
- compose a limerick

1 The first part of the lesson has your students determining the reasonableness of seven statements. Four of them are reasonable and three are not. There are a couple that might cause your students to argue with us.

Because one or two of the statements in the exercise are subject to conjecture and interpretation—we hope there will be some controversy concerning the statements, thus ensuring some thinking and further inquiry—the following "answers" should be tentatively regarded as the correct ones: 1, 3, 4, and 5 are reasonable; 2, 6, and 7 are not. For example, after an earthquake a sundial can be in error, but the amount of time it is in error will change during the day. The statement about Marion and Clair is deliberately designed to trick your students, but it might not because so many girls are called Whitney, Kendall, and Lindsay, names formerly given to boys. It is hoped that some of your students will see the trap in the statement about the woman who is suspicious of everyone who wears a bow tie, namely, that there is a difference between an illogical woman and an illogical statement; any number of people have behaved in just this unreasonable way.

2 After testing the reasonableness of the seven statements in the initial exercise, your students should be able to compose logical and illogical statements. The chance to "play teacher" appeals greatly to some students. Others like to see if they can out-think their classmates. If you decide to make this a class activity, you might have each of your students read the statement that she or he believes to be most unreasonable to the class. In this way, everyone will have an opportunity to show what she or he can do, and the class will have additional practice in testing the logic of statements. There is no need for discussion after every statement read, however; you can make the decisions about which ones are worth analyzing.

3 Limericks lend themselves to light-hearted looks at absurd and irrational behavior. Now that the students have analyzed statements as reasonable or unreasonable, end the lesson by inviting students to write a limerick. We have provided a model, but you might want to quote a famous limerick and point out the rhyme scheme and rhythm of it. Limericks are fun to write and not hard to make up. Some of the best ones come with a surprise or twist at the end.

Is It Reasonable?

Name _____   **Date** _____

❶ As you grow older you will find it increasingly important to tell the differences between statements that are reasonable and those that are incorrect or misleading. This exercise will help you to develop the ability to see how reasonable and unreasonable statements differ. Read the sentences below and decide whether or not they make sense. If you believe a sentence is reasonable, write an **R** in the space to the left of the sentence. If you believe it is unreasonable, write a **U** to the left of the sentence. Consider each statement carefully before you write an answer.

_____ 1. Gordon was the kind of boy who did everything well; he seldom played chess, but when he did, he always won.

_____ 2. Ever since the earthquake, Mr. Jensen's sundial has been one-half hour slow.

_____ 3. Marion and Clair were never sorry that they joined the Boys Glee Club.

_____ 4. Ms. Smith was suspicious of everyone who wore a bow tie because she had once seen a movie in which the villain wore a red bow tie.

_____ 5. Occasional gusts of wind blew over the desert sands, causing the hikers to unpack and put on their goggles.

_____ 6. Tom's bicycle was unusual in that the third wheel had a diameter that was 3 inches smaller than the others.

_____ 7. For nearly two years Jerry had read the financial page of the newspaper; and this habit, of course, enabled him to become an expert on stock market trends.

❷ Perhaps you can think of some additional statements that might be either reasonable or illogical. Write them below and maybe later use them to stump your classmates.

_____

_____

_____

_____

Name _____ Date _____

Which of your sentences were the most fun for others to figure out?

_____

_____

Why were they especially good?

_____

_____

_____

_____

3 Here is a limerick about the statement concerning Ms. Smith. As you know, the limerick is a humorous verse that has five lines. The first two lines rhyme with the fifth, and the third and fourth lines also rhyme.

> **Old Ms. Smith attended a show**
> **Where the villain's red tie was a bow.**
> **Ever after she cried**
> **When a bow tie she spied:**
> **"I just know that guy will cause woe!"**

Make up your own limerick based on one of the sentences in activity 1 and write it in the space below.

_____

_____

_____

_____

_____

Lesson 6

Cages

Writing a Description

About the Lesson

A cage is not an attractive concept. It connotes confinement and restraint. The first image we have when we see or hear the word is an animal in a place with bars or a songbird in a cage. *Trap* is not as unattractive to our sensibilities as is *cage*, although many animals suffer as much or more from traps. We can trap shoot, trap a criminal, trap an idea, and so forth. When we cage something, whether human or nonhuman, we take away its freedom and dignity.

Once students have begun to think rather seriously about the idea of a cage (to many people it is highly repugnant), you can administer the activity, which is probably best done individually, rather than by the entire class. Because it requires some genuine thinking, it is not a particularly easy lesson, but it can be a rewarding one if your students are in a mood to use their minds.

Targeted Learner Outcomes

The student will

- examine the concept of *cage*,
- identify which of twelve items are cages,
- explain the relationship between time and cages, and
- write a paragraph describing a cage.

1 Probably the simplest and best way to introduce this lesson is to present a cage to your students. One of moderate size would be appropriate—a bird cage or a rabbit hutch would be ideal. Most animal cages are made of wire mesh or have bars of metal or wood. The kind of cage with bars is the type we used to see at zoos and is now becoming less common as zoos are abandoning that way of confining animals. You might also describe a cage without naming it and then see if your students can guess what it is. Your description should have the essentials: an enclosed space, no way to escape (except by permission), and restricted movement.

2 At the second level students are to consider whether *time* has anything to do with whether something is a cage or not. In some cages the duration of time does determine whether it is a cage or not, as with the self-imposed isolation that people sometimes inflict upon themselves.

3 The lesson culminates in a writing activity in which your students are to choose a cage with which they are familiar and describe it—without naming it. Have them describe what they think restricts them or keeps them "caged." Then ask them to trade their descriptions with another classmate. Have students guess what the cage is.

Following Through

Encourage any inclination to follow up this lesson. Poems, stories, plays, lyrics for songs, and limericks are possibilities. In addition, some students may want to dig more deeply into the topic and do some research. Your students may also remember stories that feature cages. Encourage them to tell the stories to their classmates. There is much to be learned in the art of retelling a story.

Cages

ACTIVITY

Name _____ Date _____

❶ Have you ever thought much about *cages*? What do we put into cages?

_____

_____

Which of these items might be considered a cage?

1. an office
2. an automobile
3. a warren
4. a play pen

5. a museum
6. a gymnasium
7. a ticket window
8. a stage

9. the Earth
10. a phone booth
11. a jail
12. a sideshow

List the cages among the items above—and any others that you can think of. Then indicate what each item cages.

Cage   **Caged**

_____

_____

_____

_____

_____

_____

_____

_____

_____

_____

ACTIVITY

Name _____ Date _____

2 Does *time* have anything to do with whether something is a cage or not? What makes something a cage?

_____

_____

_____

3 In two or three paragraphs, describe a cage with which you are quite familiar. Don't name the cage—just describe it. After you have finished your description, either read it aloud or give it to a classmate to see if anyone can identify the cage. Remember that a paragraph has these features:

1. It has a topic sentence that leads off the paragraph and tells what the paragraph is about.

2. That topic is developed through details, incidents or examples, comparisons, reasons, causes, results, or effects, and/or a list of steps in a process.

3. Sentences are arranged so that the reader can move easily from one sentence to the next.

4. A concluding sentence summarizes or ties together the ideas expressed in the paragraph.

Use the space below for a first draft of your description.

_____

_____

_____

_____

_____

_____

_____

Lesson 7
More or Less
Writing a Description

About the Lesson

This lesson gets students thinking about holes—in general, places where something used to be. After some exploration about various kinds of holes, students will write a description of a hole they know.

Targeted Learner Outcomes

The student will:

- explore the concept of *hole*,
- tell about making holes, and
- describe a favorite hole.

1 If you think about how holes are formed, it is obvious that a hole can be a portion of something that was taken away or it can be created because something was built around it. The crater of a volcano is made when a portion of the mountain erupts and is blown away. On the other hand, when a student makes a volcano in the classroom, he or she is shaping material so that a hole remains. Nature does it one way, and most students do it the other way. (A few do it nature's way, too, by blowing off the tops of model volcanoes.)

Lead into the lesson with a short demonstration. Curl your fingers to make an opening, as some people do when they try to make a cup of their hands to drink from a stream. Or, with a piece of paper and a pair of scissors, cut out holes for eyes and a nose.

After your introduction, students will probably have no difficulty with this part of the lesson. They may come up with some variations, such as *cone* or *gap* for *crater* and *cavity* or *ditch* for *pit*, but they should have no trouble coming up with the answers or examples of other holes.

2 At this level the activity becomes more personal as you ask students about their experiences at making holes. Two items—an animal and a window—might be considered antisocial or negative, but the responses to these two items are likely to be more spontaneous and honest than with any of the other items.

3 The purpose in asking students to tell why they like a certain hole is to get them to describe it *and* give reasons why they favor it. Their choices might range from a gopher hole to a cave to a basketball hoop. Encourage them to examine their choices carefully. Those that want to illustrate their writing should do so, but keep the emphasis on finding the words to express ideas.

More or Less

Name _____   Date _____

1 A hole is a place that was and isn't a place any longer, such as the top of a volcano. Do you know the name of this large hole? What is it called?

_____

Does nature produce any other holes similar to this one? _____

_____

Name some. _____

_____

What is the name of the hole where there are mining operations?

_____

Name some other kinds of excavations. _____

_____

A hole is also a place that is and wasn't before, such as an underground passage for people.

Can you name this kind of hole? _____

What do we call something such as this when an animal builds it?

_____

Who is the architect of a hole that is a trap for unwary insects? _____

_____

Do you know of any hole under water that serves the same purpose?

What is it? _____

Name _____   Date _____

2 When you were younger, did you enjoy making holes? _____

Did you ever make holes in:

a curtain? _____   gum? _____

a balloon? _____   a window? _____

a test paper? _____   mud? _____

a screen door? _____   a sock? _____

a sweater? _____   sand? _____

a pudding? _____   an animal? _____

What kinds of things *can't* you make permanent holes in?

_____

_____

3 What is your favorite kind of hole? _____

Describe it and tell why you like it best.

_____

_____

_____

_____

_____

_____

Crazy Cats and Dirty Dogs

Composing a Paragraph with Alliteration

About the Lesson

This lesson mostly consists of a game featuring alliteration and an invitation for students to write a paragraph using alliterative expressions. The game is similar to a game called *hinky-pinky*, but the answers are alliterative phrases instead of rhyming words. After some practice writing alliterative phrases, students will write a paragraph containing two or more examples.

Targeted Learner Outcomes

The student will:

- understand what alliteration is,
- devise alliterative phrases that are synonymous with a dozen expressions,
- provide one alliterative expression that is equal to another, and
- write a paragraph that contains two or more examples of alliteration.

1 To introduce the lesson, go over the definition of alliteration at the top of the page. Emphasize that *alliteration* refers to words starting with the same sound. "Charming chum" is alliterative. Although the words *calm* and *celebration* both begin with a *c*, they have different beginning sounds and are not examples of alliteration.

2 Here are some alliterative expressions for the dozen items given:

1. A frisky young dog is a *peppy puppy*.

2. A brave police officer is a *courageous cop*.

3. A stingy minister is a *penny-pinching parson*.

4. A lovely flower a *pretty posey*.

5. An illustrious aviator is a *famous flyer*.

6. A fastidious man is a *meticulous male*.

7. A rowdy young man is a *boisterous boy*.

8. A terrible writer is an *awful author*.

9. An irascible young cat is a *cantankerous kitten*.

10. A sad-faced medic is a *dour doctor*.

11. A happy, upbeat friend is a *cheerful chum*.

12. A frightened rascal is a *scared scamp*.

3 Students end the lesson by composing a paragraph containing at least two alliterative expressions. By the time they reach this point, your students should be mentally prepared to write a number of alliterations. They aren't as addictive as rhymes, but once you start using the device it seems to come easily.

Crazy Cats and Dirty Dogs

ACTIVITY

Name _____   Date _____

❶ Alliteration is the repetition of the initial sound of two or more words that are close together. Which of these expressions is truly alliterative: "calm celebration" or "charming chum"? Alliteration often crops up in our speech. For example, two of our favorite animals are the subjects of these alliterative expressions: "crazy cats" and "dirty dogs."

❷ Make each of the following phrases into an alliterative expression. You may want to use a dictionary.

1. a frisky young dog _____

2. a brave police officer _____

3. a stingy minister _____

4. a lovely flower _____

5. an illustrious aviator _____

6. a fastidious man _____

7. a rowdy young man _____

8. a terrible writer _____

9. an irascible young cat _____

10. a sad-faced medic _____

11. a happy, upbeat friend _____

12. a frightened rascal _____

❸ Now, let's test your skill in writing alliterative expressions. On a separate piece of paper, write at least one paragraph about your favorite celebrity that contains two or more examples of alliteration.

License Plate Quickies

Writing a Paragraph

About the Lesson

This lesson offers students some real brainstretching fun with license plate messages. They will translate particular sets of letters and numbers from license plates into possible sentences. Then they will write a paragraph based on their license plate "translations."

Before giving "License Plate Quickies" to your students, try to do one or two of the items yourself. The lesson could be too much of a challenge for some of your students.

Targeted Learner Outcomes

The student will:

- produce sentences for seven license plate numbers, and
- take one of the sentences and put it in a paragraph.

1 When conducting this lesson, give students seven, eight, or ten minutes. It is a good idea to place a limit on the time they have and thus make it more like a game.

To give you an idea of how one mind played with the license plate numbers, these are some possible reactions to the numbers:

RWB 422   Red, white, and blue are colors found in 422 dresses at Macy's.

PKU 266   Plastic kitchen utensils broken in our house number 266 at last count.

FNS 482   Fresh noodle soup was served at Jake's Restaurant last month 482 times.

SCL 114   Silvia coughed loudly 114 times (without covering her mouth).

DGG 601   Darned good guys in our town who like soccer number at least 601.

ANA 974   Alvin never ages. He's now 974.

TJI 853   Tearful Jane Ingle's badge number at Elmer's Onion Works is 853. She's the Chief Slicer.

One of the difficult parts of translating the license numbers in this way is in writing complete sentences.

2 The task at the end of the unit is challenging. Students are to add one or two sentences to their translations to make a paragraph. It is assumed that (a) they have written complete sentences and (b) they know how to construct a paragraph. If they are not adept at composing paragraphs, it will be up to you to decide whether a lesson in paragraphing is necessary.

Following Through

If your students are in need of further instruction about writing paragraphs, you can remind them that, generally speaking, a paragraph is a unit of written communication containing sentences that are closely related in structure and meaning. The subject, or main idea, may be expressed implicitly or explicitly, but if the subject is stated explicitly, it will generally appear in the form of a topic sentence.

ACTIVITY

Name _____   Date _____

1 For many years people have played games by reading the license plates of the cars they see on the road. One of the most popular games is finding the letters of the alphabet on license plates, starting with A and ending the game with Z. Jim, whose ideas are sometimes considered strange by his friends, thought of a more challenging game while he was staring at the license plate of the car in front of him. It read QMG 490. With a little effort, Jim said to himself, "Quick Mike Geary was the last person to end the road race, and they gave him number 490."

"Ah," Jim thought, "I can do that with any license plate I see on this street." Well, he tried, but it took him longer for some plates than for others to come up with one or two sentences based on the letters and numbers. Here are the other plates that he saw:

KT DT	**SCL 114**
RWB 422	**DGG 601**
PKU 266	**ANA 974**
FNS 482	**TJI 853**

Except for the first plate, KT DT, they all had three letters followed by three numerals. Jim's reaction to "KT DT" was: "Kate 'told' but Don 'tattled'."

How many of the other plates can you make into one or two sentences in *five minutes*? If you get more than a couple, you'll be doing quite well.

RWB 422 _____

_____

PKU 266 _____

_____

FNS 482 _____

_____

SCL 114 _____

_____

From *Time to Write*, Copyright © Good Year Books. This page may be reproduced for classroom use only by the actual purchaser of the book. www.goodyearbooks.com.

License Plate Quickies (continued)

Name _____   Date _____

DGG 601 _____

_____

ANA 974 _____

_____

TJI 853 _____

_____

2 Choose one of the sentences and add two or more sentences to it to make a paragraph. If you'd like, draw a scene to illustrate your writing.

_____

_____

_____

_____

_____

_____

_____

_____

He Nobbled When He Should Have Trizzed

Writing a Paragraph with New Vocabulary Words

About the Lesson

This lesson might well precede a writing activity such as a story or a poem. It asks students to think about the words they use and to acquire new words for their vocabularies.

Targeted Learner Outcomes

The student will:

- substitute appropriate words for contrived words in a paragraph, and
- incorporate three new vocabulary words in a paragraph.

❶ The first level plunges the student right into a warm-up activity that involves figuring out an unfamiliar word's meaning from its context. Have them read the story and then ask volunteers to each name a word that is unfamiliar. Students will probably find some of the strange words humorous.

There are six words in the story that need substitutes. Not all students will suggest the same new words, so allow discussion time. This will add new words to all students' vocabularies.

Norton the Great

Norton was a great athlete, but this time he just *nobbled* (bobbled or muffed) the ball. People always expected him to *trizz* (shine or excel), as he usually did in quite a dazzling way. No one in the stands was more unhappy for Norton than his father, who was terribly *vorced* (concerned). Because he'd played baseball as a *yop* (boy or young man) himself, Norton's father knew that there were times when you are playing that you feel like crawling under a big *geon* (rock). He only wished that this *mithry* (painful or excrutiating) moment would pass as quickly as possible.

❷ The last part of the lesson should be administered after students complete the first part. (There may be a lively discussion about the made-up words in the story and about made-up words in general.) It requires that your students record words that are new to them and to list the words and their definitions. Unless your students have already done an activity like this, they will need to be aware of unknown words that they encounter for at least a day or two. For those of your students who can make associations easily, writing a paragraph incorporating three of the ten words will be easy. Others may find it difficult, but there is no reason why they can't do some imaginative thinking and make the connections.

He Nobbled When He Should Have Trizzed

ACTIVITY

Name _____ Date _____

1 The following story includes a number of strange words. Read the story
and try to guess the meaning of any word you don't know, based on the
context. Then rewrite the story, using appropriate words in place of the
strange ones. Make the substituted words as colorful and effective as you
can. You can use a dictionary or thesaurus to help you find suitable words.

Norton the Great

Norton was a great athlete, but this time he just nobbled the
ball. People always expected him to trizz, as he usually did in
quite a dazzling way. No one in the stands was more unhappy
for Norton than his father, who was terribly vorced. Because
he'd played baseball as a yop himself, Norton's father knew
that there were times when you are playing that you feel like
crawling under a big geon. He only wished that this mithry
moment would pass as quickly as possible.

Norton the Great (rewritten)

_____

_____

_____

_____

_____

_____

_____

_____

_____

_____

ACTIVITY

Name _____   Date _____

2 Compile a list of ten words that you have encountered recently that were not in your speaking or writing vocabularies and give the definition of each of those words. When you have compiled your list, choose three and incorporate them into a paragraph about a topic that they suggest to you. For example, if you had found ten worthwhile words to add to your vocabulary that included *placid*, *vortex*, and *prescient*, you might think of a quiet fortune teller who predicts that a small boat will be lost in a whirlpool! Write your paragraph on a separate sheet of paper.

New Words for My Vocabulary

      Word   **Definition**

1. _____

2. _____

3. _____

4. _____

5. _____

6. _____

7. _____

8. _____

9. _____

10. _____

Lesson 11

Working Over Language

Recognizing Clichés

About the Lesson

As the title of this lesson suggests, most of us—young and old alike—work over the same expressions until, if they are not beaten up, they are very tired. Thus at some point in the school year you'll probably need to remind students about the pitfalls of overworked expressions, or clichés.

Targeted Learner Outcomes

The student will:

- supply five current adjectives for the ones that were overworked in 1964, and
- write a paragraph in which every sentence contains a cliché and then replace the clichés with less trite expressions.

1 Students will turn up their noses at all five of the expressions from 1964, calling them weird. Students may not know what the expressions mean. Emphasize that these were popular overused expressions in everyday language in the mid-1960s.

Teachers have been crying out against students using tired, predictable language for ages. Therefore, this lesson can be regarded as a traditional lesson about avoiding hackneyed language and using fresher and less predictable expressions. You don't have to administer this lesson in a traditional way, though. You can break up your class into small groups of three and four and have them discuss the five sentences.

2 The five old clichés may or may not induce a few chuckles from students but then you might point out that in fifty years the ones they choose to replace *grand*, *divine*, and the others may cause other young people to laugh at their expressions.

3 As students write their cliché-riddled paragraphs, remind them that every sentence should contain at least one overused expression. When students start their second paragraph, remind them of the warning about exchanging one cliché for another. Students may still end up with some clichés simply because they don't really understand what a cliché is and how very often they use hackneyed expressions ("That's just the way we talk."). Accordingly, this section of the exercise is by far the most important, and it should prove to be the most interesting. You can go over the paragraphs of several willing students and discuss how well they have avoided clichés and instead used fresh language. Maybe not one of your students will substitute one cliché for another!

Following Through

You may find that students don't agree about what constitutes a cliché. Compile a class list of those expressions that a majority of the class agrees are overworked. Refer to this list from time to time during the year to see if students have changed their thinking about particular expressions.

Working Over Language

ACTIVITY

Name _____   Date _____

❶   The party was divine.

Isn't he keen?

We had a grand time.

She looked dragged-out.

The movie was super.

Do these sentences sound strange to you? Well, in 1964 a language expert called those adjectives—*divine, keen, grand, dragged-out,* and *super*—stale and overworked. Do you ever hear anyone use any of them now? If so, which ones?

_____

_____

❷   Can you give a more up-to-date expression for each of the adjectives in the five sentences above? Choose words that are used all of the time by your friends and acquaintances.

divine = _____

keen = _____

grand = _____

dragged-out = _____

super = _____

Name _____   **Date** _____

3 Overworked expressions are called *clichés*. They also include phrases such as "shaking like a leaf," "breathtaking view," "back to the wall," and "sells like hotcakes." When you know what's coming after hearing only the first one or two words, you know you are listening to a cliché.

Write a paragraph in which *every* sentence contains a cliché.

_____

_____

_____

_____

_____

_____

_____

Now, rewrite your paragraph so that all of the clichés are removed. Be careful, though—you may be substituting one cliché for another.

_____

_____

_____

_____

_____

_____

_____

"How to Start a Car"

Writing Advertisements

About the Lesson

In several ways this lesson requires some sophisticated thinking. Students must visualize an advertisement in a business magazine and then manage to write some catchy headings for seven products. Although they are asked only to write the headings and not the copy, the task is challenging and may take an entire class period.

Targeted Learner Outcome

The student will:

- write eye-catching headings for ads for seven diverse products.

1 Write the heading "How to start a car," on the board. Explain that this is a heading from an ad in a business magazine. Ask students to think about what that ad might be about. What kind of company placed the ad? Ask students to write predictions on this part of their paper. Although the answer is given in the next paragraph, ask students to make a guess nonetheless.

2 Suggest to students that they come up with several headings for each of the products and services before deciding on the best ones. In fact, this is often how a group of copywriters works when composing an effective ad.

Have students use these criteria as guides for writing their ad headlines:

1. Does the heading get your attention?

2. Does the heading have a simple message?

3. Is the heading appropriate for the readers of the magazine, the ones the product is meant to attract?

4. Will the heading lead naturally into whatever copy might follow?

Probably the best way to evaluate students' headings is to use your own judgment about what is appropriate, eye-catching, and effective in ads of this kind.

"How to Start a Car"

Name _____   Date _____

❶ Headline seen in an ad in a business magazine:

"How to start a car"

What do you suppose was the text of the ad, and what corporation was the ad written for?

_____

_____

❷ Copywriters have the challenging task of capturing our attention first and then delivering a clever, compelling message in order to convince us to buy their product or service. It's not an easy job because there are many, many ads competing for our attention. In the case of the ad cited above, the pitch was for a "freight transportation partner," Consolidated Freightways. It might have been for an auto parts maker or a driver training course. The ad's two pages contained photographs of keys (hanging from the "a" in the heading); an engine; a spark plug; and the key image, one of CF's trucks.

Why don't you try your hand at copywriting? Come up with catchy headings for the following products and services. They should be related directly to an imagined text and art for the ad. Do some research about each of the products and services before you write your headings.

Product or Service	Heading
1. preschool toys	_____
2. motor oil	_____
3. ladies evening footwear	_____
4. a Bermuda resort	_____
5. fountain pens (which use ink)	_____
6. an employment agency that finds jobs for executives	_____
	_____
7. a catering service	_____

Lesson 13

Opportunity Calls
Composing Advertisements

About the Lesson
Although the Internet seems to have become the best way for advertisers to reach large groups of potential customers, this lesson harkens back to the less advanced mode of selling on the radio. Because of transistor and car radios, programs such as that described in the lesson can still be heard throughout the land.

Targeted Learner Outcomes
The student will:
- give two pieces of information essential to any radio advertisements, and
- write an advertisement to sell an unwanted item on the radio.

1 The introduction asks students to imagine that they live in a small town where inhabitants are fans of a radio program that advertises, without charge, items for sale. If your students live in a city or urban area, explain the popularity of such programs and their importance in the life of a small town.

2 Help students understand that the two pieces of information that must be included in every ad presented on the radio program are the price of the item to be sold and the telephone number (or address) of the seller.

3 Students must compose an advertisement in only twenty-five words. Before they start, tell them to first jot down the essential characteristics of the item for sale and the principal reasons anyone would want to buy it. These points can be the basis for the ad.

Following Through

This lesson may have a practical application for your students. The school's student newspaper may have a "For Sale" section—or, if not, one can be inaugurated. For more detailed advertisements, you can give your students this advice from a professional copywriter:

- Use "power" words when you write. For example, *rich* is better than *wealthy*. *Gossip* and *chat* have more power than *talk*.

- The sound of words is important—onomatopoeia, alliteration, cadence, and a strong use of consonants tend to help the way your phrases and sentences sound. Rhythm is very important.

- Write the way people talk. If you have to consult a thesaurus, so will your audience. The famous copywriter John Caples said that in one ad he changed a word from *repair* (an expert kind of thing) to *fix* (a layman kind of thing), and the ad pulled a 20-percent better response.

- Know your audience. Who are you trying to reach?

- Puns are fine, but don't overuse them. Sometimes they can draw attention away from the product you are selling.

Opportunity Calls

ACTIVITY

Name _____   Date _____

① Let's imagine that you live in a small town where many people listen each weekday afternoon to a local disk jockey who announces a lot of local news. Among the regular features on the disk jockey's program is "Opportunity Calls," a time in which he gives free advertisements for items people want to sell. Anyone can write to him and give the details of the item for sale. He prefers that people mail their information because phoning in ads would clog up the station's phone lines.

② The disk jockey has quite a few ads to read every day, and so he restricts the length of the ads to twenty-five words. What two pieces of information must be included in any ad sent to the disk jockey?

1. _____

2. _____

Let's also imagine that you have something you no longer need and would like some extra money. Perhaps it is a pair of skates, a bicycle, a portable radio, a toy, a computer, or a pet from a new litter. Think of something you have that you might sell, or imagine something that you'd like to sell. What is it?

_____

③ How would you word your ad to make sure your item will appeal to the radio audience in the allotted twenty-five words? Remember: There are two pieces of information that he needs about you and your item or he won't read your ad on the air. Write your first and second drafts in the space below.

_____

_____

_____

_____

_____

_____

Lesson 14

Not a Whiner

Writing a Letter to the Editor

About the Lesson

The lesson begins with a letter to the editor that was written by the captain of a high school football team. It ends with an invitation to write a letter to the editor of the local newspaper, along with tips for writing an effective letter to the editor.

Targeted Learner Outcomes

The student will:

- assess the positions of two individuals in writing letters to the editor, and
- write a letter to the editor.

1 Start the lesson with a discussion of newspaper op-ed pages and the role of letters to the editor on those pages. Bring in some examples to share. Mention that every local newspaper has a few avid letter writers, faithful readers who write more often than other people. If necessary, go over proper letter form with students, using the lesson's example as a model.

2 At the next level, students are asked who they believe is essentially telling the true story—Jesse Silva or Loren Alderson.

3 In many small towns and medium-sized cities young people do write letters to the editor, and so to expect some of your students to send their letters to a newspaper isn't far-fetched. If they follow the suggestions for writing the letter, chances are good that their letters will appear in print.

ACTIVITY

Name _____   Date _____

1   The following letter was written in response to a letter sent to the editor of a local newspaper concerning the disreputable behavior of high school students at a football game.

October 30, 2007

To the Editor:

    Nearly everyone I've talked with has disagreed with Loren Alderson's biased comments in the October 11 edition of the paper about the behavior of Piner's students during the Garfield game. I personally know of no Piner student who "hurled epithets" at the visiting Garfield High players when they left our field.

    When the referee's decision gave Garfield an extra down on the five-yard line and allowed them to score the winning touchdown, our coaches protested, but not one of our players swore at the ref or at Garfield's players. I was on the field and I know what I'm talking about. We are not, as Mr. Alderson accused us, a bunch of "Whiners from Piner." My friends and my family were in the stands, and they saw no incidents of our students taunting the Garfield players or students. Could it be that Mr. Alderson has been listening to people who have always had it in for Piner?

    If Mr. Alderson can cite one incident of bad sportsmanship, witnessed by reliable witnesses, I'll apologize in person for that behavior. I call for a total apology from Mr. Alderson for his prejudiced remarks.

Jesse Silva
92 Sherman St.

2   The letter writer had three members of his family and two friends read his letter before he mailed it to the newspaper.

Jesse Silva was captain of the football team at Piner High School at the time he wrote his letter. Loren Alderson is a retired businessman. Which person do you tend to believe—Mr. Alderson or Jesse Silva?

_____

Why? _____

_____

_____

ACTIVITY

Name _____ Date _____

3 A large proportion of subscribers to a small-town newspaper read the Letters to the Editor page. It is a good forum for the different viewpoints of the community, and editors pay attention to what their readers are writing. If you have something that you want to say to your community, why don't you compose a letter to the editor and send it to the newspaper? If you don't feel an urge to express a viewpoint or raise an issue, think of a topic that is dear to your heart and write a letter to the editor, just for practice; there may be a time when you are concerned enough to write one.

When writing a letter to the editor, keep in mind that the letters column of a newspaper or magazine gives readers a chance to express opinions and to share information. Although the letters are addressed to the editor, they really are meant to be read by everyone in the publication's audience.

To write a letter to the editor:

1. Choose a topic. Many letters to the editor are about stories and columns that have appeared in the publication or about a letter written by another reader. These letters usually involve a strong opinion.

2. Summarize your main point in a single sentence. Doing so will help you write a letter that is clear and strong. An example would be: "We should have more soccer fields because we don't have enough to accommodate all of our teams."

3. Draft the letter. When drafting your letter, you might:

   • summarize the article or topic your letter will deal with.

   • tell about yourself and why the topic matters to you.

   • give your opinion about the topic.

   • give information that will interest other readers.

   • describe an action that readers can take to support your ideas. An example would be asking the city manager about illegal signs in the business district.

4. Test the letter. Ask a trial reader for suggestions that might make the letter clearer or more forceful.

5. Polish the letter and then mail it. Most publications require that you include your home phone number. In this way they can call you to make sure that you are the person who wrote the letter.

6. Read the publication to see if your letter was printed. Later, see if anyone responds to what you wrote. You might then write a follow-up letter that further explains your idea.

Lesson 15
Riddles in Time
Composing Riddles

About the Lesson

Children love riddles. *Highlights for Children* magazine publishes a popular monthly feature in which youngsters can contribute original riddles. In this lesson students will puzzle over a group of riddles and then write some of their own.

Targeted Learner Outcomes

The student will:

- provide solutions for seven riddles, and
- compose two or more riddles.

1 Give students enough time to think and answer the riddles on the lesson page. Emphasize that some riddles may have more than one possible answer. For example, the fourth riddle about the similarity of a clock and a parent can have several answers, and the last riddle about the country dog and the old clock might also have a punny answer instead of "ticks."

These are acceptable answers to the seven riddles about time:

1. The hands of a clock very rarely stay together, even when the clock has stopped.

2. Time.

3. Cheryl was talking to her daughter on the telephone, and her daughter was in a different time zone.

4. When they get wound up, a parent and a clock go on for a long time.

5. Time.

6. The conductor beats time.

7. Ticks.

2 The lesson ends with an invitation to students to compose their own riddles. Although this activity would seem to be better suited to young children, intermediate-age students will find it challenging.

Modern-day riddles are most often based on a play on words. Thus, puns are very popular in riddles. For example, if you give an example, such as "Who has the easiest job in the world?" (a candle maker—he only has to work on wick ends), students can catch on to one way of making up riddles. Have students exchange their riddles in order to stump each other, and include the riddles in student publications.

Riddles in Time

Name _____   Date _____

❶ The riddles below all relate to time in some way. See if you can solve them.

1. What two things meet regularly but almost never stay together?

2. What goes slower when we are in trouble but faster as we grow older?

3. Why did Cheryl say to her daughter, "Good morning, honey," when the clock on her VCR read 9:00 P.M.?

4. Why are a clock and a parent alike?

5. What can be divided but never conquered?

6. What crime does a conductor commit when conducting a band?

7. What does a miserable country dog have in common with an old clock?

❷ Make up a couple of riddles. They don't have to be about time.

_____

_____

_____

_____

_____

_____

Punny Riddles

Composing Riddles

About the Lesson

This is a simple lesson in simple humor. No matter how much and how often some people criticize riddles, young people still like them. This lesson offers a dozen assorted riddles that depend upon puns for their humor. Students also get to concoct their own riddles.

Targeted Learner Outcomes

The student will:

- solve a dozen riddles,
- recall three difficult riddles, and
- make up three riddles.

1 Here are possible answers to the twelve riddles:

1. When it is reddy / ready

2. He didn't knead / need it.

3. In the barn next to Pa's cow

4. Retire

5. For his Punch 'n' Judy

6. They have lots of scare cases.

7. "Oh dear / deer!"

8. A lighthouse

9. With 22 carrots and a lot of bullion

10. He'd gotten a birdie.

11. An airplane (Orville and Wilbur Wright/"right")

12. When you do it right, you get an abadile. When you do it wrong, you get a crocobalone.

2 At the next level, we ask your students to recall the three funniest riddles that they have heard. Although every one of your students may not be able to remember three riddles, all of them should be able to recall at least one.

3 This activity could prove to be an important one for any genuine wits in your class. Young people do invent riddles, as noted by E. Paul Torrance (1999):

Who was the smartest inventor and why?

Answer: Edison. He invented the phonograph so that people would stay up all night using his electric light bulbs.*

* From E. P. Torrance and H. T. Shafter, *Making the Creative Leap Beyond* (Buffalo, N.Y.: Creative Education Foundation Press, 1999), pp. 226–227.

Punny Riddles

Name _____   Date _____

1 When you were younger, you probably heard the old riddle, "When is a door not a door? When it is ajar!" That kind of riddle depends on a play on words—a pun. All riddles don't have puns, but a great many do. Here are some punny riddles that you may enjoy solving.

1. When is the best time to pick a tomato? _____

2. Why did the baker throw the extra dough away? _____

3. Where is Moscow? _____

4. What should a driver do when he has a second flat tire at night? _____

_____

5. Why was the puppeteer arrested after his performance? _____

_____

6. What do ghosts like about tall buildings? _____

7. What did the gardener say when she saw the
   leafless rose bush and hoof prints near it? _____

8. What house weighs the least? _____

9. How do you make gold soup? _____

10. Why did the golfer crow after he fired his last shot? _____

_____

11. If two wrongs don't make a right, what do two rights make? _____

_____

12. What do you get when you cross an abalone and a crocodile? _____

_____

Name _____   Date _____

2 Those riddles may have been too easy for you. Write down three of the funniest riddles you've ever heard. Use them to stump your classmates.

1. _____

_____

2. _____

_____

3. _____

_____

3 Now try to make up three more of your own. You can get ideas for punny riddles by thinking of words that sound alike but mean different things, such as *you* (*ewe*), *forth* (*fourth*), and *flew* (*flu*). Or you can think of words that are similar to one another, such as *barking/parking* and *bacon/bakin'*. Write your riddles in the space below.

_____

_____

_____

_____

_____

_____

_____

_____

_____

Lesson 17

Promises

Writing a Poem

About the Lesson

An excellent way of introducing this lesson is to invite students to discuss the signs that indicate that some event is about to happen—the "promise" of something to come. At any given moment there are signs all around us that events are about to take place. One of your students may be expecting a baby brother or sister and notice the changes in the furniture of his or her house, in the dinner conversation, and in the clothing of his or her mother. Another of your students may play a competitive sport and notice the change in herself or himself and in others as the hour of a game approaches. Still another student may notice a change in the activities of classmates as the time for dismissal gets nearer. There are certainly a variety of clues that tip us off before any event of importance takes place, and this lesson will get students thinking about these clues, or promises.

Targeted Learner Outcomes

The student will:

- understand why some events anticipate other events, and
- write a poem about a promise.

❶ The first level asks students to play a game of making associations. They are to think of what might happen after various events have taken place: the splashing of water, the spilling of milk, the click of a light switch, the humming of bees, the hissing of steam, the rustle of leaves, the grinding of a pencil in a pencil sharpener, and the rumble of a motor. Your students' responses will reflect their backgrounds and personalities. You can decide whether students should read aloud their associations; some students may not wish to share their personal feelings with others.

❷ Students do some evaluating at the second level, deciding which of the promises appeals most and which appeals least.

❸ Your students will now compose a poem. The particular form of verse is not important. However, if some students are wary of writing poetry, give them the option of writing couplets because they rhyme and the stanza is only two lines long.

Promises

Name _____ Date _____

1 Just as the sight of geese flying north is the sign of the coming spring in some places and the rush of a southern wind is the sign of an approaching rainstorm in other places, certain events give promise of what is to come. What promise do the events below hold for you personally?

Event   **Promise**

1. The splashing of water _____

Why did you think of that particular promise? _____

_____

2. The spilling of milk _____

Why did you connect that event with milk spilling? _____

_____

3. The click of a light switch _____

Why did you think of that "promise" in connection with a light switch clicking?

_____

4. The humming of bees_____

Why did you think of that "promise" with regard to bees? _____

_____

5. The hissing of steam? _____

What made you think of that "promise"? _____

_____

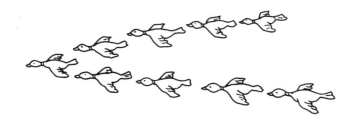

Name _____   Date _____

Event	Promise

6. The rustling of leaves? _____

Why did you think of that "promise" in connection with the rustling of leaves?

_____

7. The grinding of a pencil in a sharpener? _____

Why did you think of that particular "promise"? _____

_____

8. The rumble of a motor? _____

Why did you think of that eventuality? _____

_____

2 Which of your promises appeals most to you? Why?

_____

_____

Which of the promises appeals least to you? Why?

_____

_____

3 Take the "promise" that most appeals to you—or another sign of something to come—and write a poem about it. Think about what kind of rhythm would create the right mood for your ideas. Choose words that cause pictures to form in the minds of the people who listen to your poem. It doesn't matter whether you use a rhyme scheme or not, but try to write the lines so that they seem to work together. Most of all, try to capture the quality of your subject by using words that create the right mood. Use a separate sheet of paper to work out your ideas and write your poem.

Lesson 18

A Portrait of a Dog

Writing a Poem

About the Lesson

In this lesson a discussion of dogs leads to an invitation to write a poem. The obvious reasons for choosing dogs as the subject of the poem are the nearly universal interest in the animals and the hope that your students won't be self-conscious about the free verse-writing. In several ways, however, it is easier to imitate a certain rhyme and rhythm pattern when a student attempts to write a poem, and so this isn't necessarily an easy activity for most students.

Targeted Learner Outcomes

The student will:

- name at least four characteristics that all dogs share,
- list at least six traits of a particular dog, and
- write a poem about a dog.

1 The first part of the lesson gets students to generate some words about dogs that they can later use in their poems. Introduce the lesson with a brief discussion about the importance of dogs to humans, but try not to provide students with any particular words, such as *loyal*. Students should come up with their own dog words.

2 Next, students are asked to think about dog characteristics. Among the characteristics all dogs share are these:

1. four legs (quadruped)

2. keen sense of smell

3. keen hearing

4. high degree of intelligence

5. gobble their food as though they are keeping other animals from grabbing it

6. curl their tails between their legs when they are frightened

3 After listing characteristics of a dog they know well, students can write a free-verse poem about that dog. Have them read the lesson's sample poem to get started.

Following Through

Depending upon students' ages and backgrounds, there are other activities that accompany or follow this lesson. In the case of a poem about a particular breed of dog, a student might want to make a sketch of the subject or find a photograph or picture of the dog. Many dogs have colorful and fascinating histories, and you can encourage your students to learn more about them. The Russian Wolfhound, St. Bernard, Whippet, poodle, Pekinese, Chihuahua, Samoyed, Mastiff, and Great Dane all are dogs whose evolution and service to mankind should be fascinating to research.

As in other lessons, students' poems can be displayed or included in student publications.

A Portrait of a Dog

ACTIVITY

Name _____ Date _____

1 We have a lot of expressions concerning dogs, such as:

He leads a dog's life.

That dirty dog!

I wouldn't give that to a dog.

Doggone it!

This town is going to the dogs.

He's sick as a dog.

We dogged Uncle Jack's heels
all day long.

Barking dogs never bite.

Every dog has his day.

Let sleeping dogs lie.

You can't teach an old dog new tricks.

That's like letting the tail wag the dog.

Hot diggity dog!

Because dogs are so frequently found in our speech, they must be
prominent in our thinking. As a matter of fact, dogs were the very first
animal to be tamed by humans, and they have proved to be invaluable in
work, play, and sport. They herd animals, guard our homes, act as canine
police, guide the blind, perform in theaters and circuses, pull sleds, and
are invaluable companions. If you had only one word to describe dogs,
what would it be? _____

What two other words would you use to describe your favorite dog?

_____

2 Dogs come in a great variety of sizes, colors, coats, and temperaments,
but all of them share some characteristics. Name at least four of
these characteristics.

1. _____

2. _____

3. _____

4. _____

Name _____ **Date** _____

3 Think about a dog you know well or particularly like.

What is its name? _____ Is it male or female? _____

Now think of several traits of this dog. All dogs have a personality, just as humans do, whether it is happy, playful, sickly, aggressive, strong, cowardly, fierce, high-strung, timid, and so on. Below, name a half-dozen of these traits.

1. _____

2. _____

3. _____

4. _____

5. _____

6. _____

With those traits in mind, write a verse about the dog. The verse doesn't have to rhyme. It should give the reader a vivid picture of the dog's physical appearance and its personality. Write a rough draft, attempting to put words on paper that clearly portray the dog. Then look at your rough draft critically. You may see some words that need changing, or you may want to alter the rhythm of a line. Give it to a classmate to read and ask for comments. With those comments to guide you, write a final draft of your verse.

Following is an example of a verse about dogs that was written in just this way:

> A dog is a lithe athlete leaping high in the air for a ball or Frisbee®,
>
> A combination vacuum cleaner and panhandler lurking near the dinner table,
>
> An indignant policeman keeping the area clear of haughty cats,
>
> A cold, moist nose on a sweltering day,
>
> A sympathetic tongue on your fresh wound,
>
> That happy bark you hear as you come home after a dreadful day.

Now write your poem on a separate sheet of paper.

Lesson 19

Traces

Writing a Haiku

About the Lesson

This lesson will lead students into a verse-writing activity based on some thinking about "traces." Traces, in general, are things left behind, such as a footprint, after an event. The more mental energy students bring to bear on the pre-writing activities, the richer their writing will be.

Targeted Learner Outcomes

The student will:

- understand *trace* as a useful concept,
- understand the form and feeling of a haiku, and
- write a haiku based on the phrases.

1 At this first level, invite students to think about the kinds of things that indicate an event has taken place. Explain that you want them to think about "traces," things left behind by an assortment of other things, such as those listed on the student page. Ask students to volunteer some examples to assess their understanding of the concept. Then let them get started on the lesson page. Notice that the items at the beginning of the list on the student page tend to evoke images of physical objects. These items may be easier for students who think more concretely. Several of the items are purposely ambiguous to provoke students' creativity.

2 After mentally searching for the tangible and intangible traces of the items on the list, your students are asked to think again about two of the traces. Then they are asked to construct phrases expressing the significance that one of the two traces has for themselves and others.

3 After writing phrases that communicate their thoughts about the traces, students will have the foundation for a fascinating haiku. Onitsura's haiku offers a model to get them started. If students find it difficult to turn their phrases into this type of poem, encourage them to arrange their phrases into some kind of order. This will give them a feel for creating poetry.

Following Through

If some students are still shy about writing poetry, try this lesson again (or a variation of it), substituting other items for the original ten, and see how they react. Try substituting the following in the new lesson: a family picnic, a dance, an ocean tide, an explosion, a cloud, a smile, summer, a losing football season, goodbye, and greed.

Name _____   **Date** _____

1 A trace is evidence left behind after something has happened. A trace can be as visible as a snail's trail on the pavement in the morning or the white, smoky contrail of a jet airplane that has passed overhead. Some traces, however, are not so obvious. A detective might have to search very hard to find a trace that can help in solving a crime.

What are the traces of each of these events?

1. a snake's travels in the desert? _____

2. a flood? _____

3. a fire in a fireplace? _____

4. an anti-aircraft barrage? _____

5. music that has been played? _____

6. someone's hand or footprint in the wet cement of a sidewalk?

_____

7. a broken promise? _____

8. a thief's fear? _____

9. a kindness? _____

10. a bitter argument? _____

Name _____   Date _____

2 Select any two of the traces you have identified and write several phrases about them. Try to paint word pictures of the traces so that others can imagine your ideas.

_____

_____

_____

_____

_____

_____

3 Now choose one of the two sets of phrases you have written and think about them. See if you can make them into one picture and write a brief poem, such as a haiku. As you probably know, there are seventeen syllables in a traditional haiku, arranged in three lines. The first line has five syllables, the second has seven syllables, and the third has five syllables. Here is an example of haiku by Uejima Onitsura, an eighteenth-century Japanese poet:

Under the rainclouds

The plum blossoms seem like stars

Despite the daylight.

A haiku is usually about nature, but in this activity your haiku can be on a subject of your choosing.

_____

_____

_____

Lesson 20

Weathergrams

Writing Weathergrams

About the Lesson

The weathergram was invented in the middle of the twentieth century by Lloyd Reynolds, a professor of English and art at Reed College in Portland, Oregon. Because Reynolds was also a master calligrapher, he wrote his weathergrams in calligraphy. Reynolds was inspired by the Shinto prayer slips that are attached to trees in Japan, and so he and his students wrote on slips of brown craft paper (often from shopping bags) and hung them on trees all over campus. Although the verse itself is reminiscent of haiku and tanka because of its brevity and nature theme, Reynolds did not imitate the Japanese verse forms. Here is a typical weathergram:

> **Fireflies beckon**
>
> > **on a moonless night**
> >
> > **bewitchingly**

In this lesson, students will learn about and write their own weathergrams.

Targeted Learner Outcomes

The student will:

- learn what a weathergram is, and
- write a weathergram.

1 Share with students the essentials of a weathergram:

- It is about nature and the weather.
- It is composed of only a sentence or a sentence fragment.
- The emphasis is upon observing and responding to nature.
- It is visual as well as aural; words are arranged on the lines for dramatic effect.
- A title is optional. (Reynolds didn't have them.)

Then go over the brief description and weathergram examples on the student page.

These are three attempts to compose weathergrams with the kind of spacing that Reynolds used:

Towers of white
                        in the east
            offer hope to a
                    parched earth

After the rain
the earthworm
            writhes
        on the sidewalk,
its home flooded

SNAILS
Silver trails
            show the way
                    to my
        choicest
                    plants

2 Because they require only a dozen words or fewer, weathergrams should appeal to your students. Have students experiment with the spacing of the words on the lines. Note that two of the examples above use single words on some lines. Ostensibly, this gives a more dramatic effect.

Successful weathergrams will paint a word picture of an event or phenomenon of nature in a few words. Nine or ten words seem to be about right, and about fourteen syllables is the average. The imagery inspired by the verse is the most important consideration in evaluating a weathergram. Important words can stand alone on a line. Your students may want to experiment with their verses to see how to arrange words and lines to produce the desired effects.

Weathergrams

Name _____ Date _____

1 A weathergram is a very brief poem about some happening in nature, especially about weather and the seasons. It is perhaps the shortest of all forms of verse. This weathergram was written in the summer:

Clear sky,

       scorched feet—

           a half-eaten hot dog

        lies in the sand

Because a weathergram is concerned with a personal experience, you can write one by focusing your thoughts about an event that particularly appealed to you. For example, the verse above recalls an experience at the beach.

Sometimes when we see dust and other materials swirling around in a dry field in the country, we say, "Oh, look—there's a whirlwind." One person thought of his experience viewing that phenomenon and wrote:

Tiny cyclones

    dancing

    on the dry

        earth—

like whirling dervishes

Notice that the words of weathergrams are arranged on the lines to give them dramatic effect. The first word is capitalized, but there is no punctuation at the end.

Name _____   Date _____

This weathergram should strike a chord in your memory:

Dry leaves

          gossip

          as the wind

            tumbles them

               past my

                  window

2 You can write a weathergram. It need only be a dozen words or fewer and a title isn't necessary. Try writing one or two weathergrams now. To get started, just think of an experience you have had out-of-doors and write about how it made you feel.

_____

_____

_____

_____

_____

_____

_____

_____

Thoughts

Writing a Cinquain

About the Lesson

This is a simple lesson that will first have students thinking of what they enjoy doing and then invite them to express their feelings about one of their favorite things in a cinquain.

Targeted Learner Outcomes

The student will:

- explore three things they enjoy,
- understand the form of a cinquain, and
- write a cinquain about something that is enjoyable.

1 The lesson starts by asking students to name three favorite things. Have them fill in the blanks provided.

2 Finally, students should write a cinquain about one of the things on their list of favorites. The example given is a cinquain with the 1-2-3-4-1 word pattern, but purists prefer the 2-4-6-8-2 syllabic pattern that Adelaide Crapsey used when she invented this miniature verse form. It's easier to teach the pattern shown here, but it is possible to combine the two, making the five lines conform to both patterns (for example, the first line would be one word but two syllables, the second would be two words of a total of four syllables, and so on).

Thoughts

Name _____   Date _____

❶ Boys and girls like all kinds of things—spiders, clowns, fishing, a game of tag, rockets, baking cakes and cookies, gum, puzzles, puppies, ice cream, reading, bikes, hikes, television, talking, and much more. But everyone doesn't like the same things. Pick three things you like most and tell why you enjoy them so much.

1. I like _____ because _____

_____

2. I like _____ because _____

_____

3. I like _____ because _____

_____

❷ Pick one of the things you enjoy most and arrange your thoughts like this:

Flakes	(one word, the subject)
Glittering, sparkling	(two words about the subject)
Softly, gently falling	(three words of action)
A cloud's frozen tear	(four words of feeling)
Snow	(another word for the subject)

This little poem of five lines, or cinquain, was written on a cold winter morning. You can see that each line has one more word than the one before, except for the last line. Cinquains can be written about almost any subject. Use the space below to write your cinquain.

_____

_____

_____

_____

_____

The Naming Business

Naming

About the Lesson

This lesson goes rather deeply into the naming business, which, in fact, *is* a business. Many companies hire other companies to come up with names for new businesses, products, and processes. Naming is really a rather serious undertaking. After spending some time thinking about names, students will be more aware of the names they give characters in their own writing.

Targeted Learner Outcomes

The student will

- learn the importance of names in written compositions,
- name a dozen people, products, and businesses,
- recall funny names, and
- list seven memorable names from movies, books, and television sitcoms.

1 It seems that very few teenagers are completely satisfied with their names, and so this lesson starts by asking if students know the stories behind their own names. Ask students to volunteer their answers here. Wind up with a discussion of the importance of names.

2 In the second part of the lesson your students are to put themselves in the role of an inventor of names. If they get really creative, they are likely to make up some interesting or humorous names. This phase of the lesson is designed to get your students to become more aware of the importance of the names for the people in their compositions.

3 The final part of the lesson asks students to recall at least seven names they have encountered in books, films, and on television that were particularly appropriate for the characters. Then they are to write the reasons why they remember the names and to note which ones were particularly appropriate for their characters. This will remind them that the names they choose for their characters are really quite important.

Following Through

A logical follow-up to the lesson involves students writing a character sketch of someone with an unusual name. Although painting a portrait in words may appear to be a relatively easy task—we describe people to others almost daily—a successful sketch depends upon a happy combination of the ability to combine words in appealing and forceful ways and a sensitivity to the traits, big and small, that differentiate one individual from another.

The Naming Business

Name _____ Date _____

1 Do you think names play important roles in the successes and failures of people or products? There have been many people who have tried to "live up" to their names, and perhaps more who have tried to "live them down." (If you know why your name was chosen, give the reason.)

_____

2 Let's see how good you are at naming different things.

1. What would be a good name for the owner of an electrical appliances store?

_____

2. What name would you give to a television show that features a teenage acrobat?

_____

3. What would be a good name for a rest home for deep-sea divers?

_____

4. What would be a good name for a bookmark that tastes like chocolate pudding?

_____

ACTIVITY

Name _____   Date _____

5. What name would you give to a shop which puts retreads on used running shoes?

_____

6. What would be an appropriate name for a steeplejack who is afraid of heights?

_____

7. What would be a good name for a man who has a terrible temper?

_____

8. What would be a good name for a hairdresser who is bald?

_____

9. What would be a good name for a restaurant that specializes in French cooking and features frog's legs and snails?

_____

10. What would be a good name for an actor who only takes the roles of crazy criminals?

_____

11. What would be a good name for a girl who has perfect pitch and sings beautifully?

_____

12. What would be a good name for a teacher who is hard of hearing?

_____

ACTIVITY

Name _____   Date _____

3 Writers usually give quite a bit of thought to naming the characters in their stories. Mark Twain, for example, must have thought Tom Sawyer, Becky Thatcher, Huckleberry Finn, Indian Joe, and Aunt Polly were particularly appropriate names for his characters in *The Adventures of Tom Sawyer*. Try to recall some of the names of characters in books, in the films, or in television sitcoms. List at least seven.

1. _____

2. _____

3. _____

4. _____

5. _____

6. _____

7. _____

What reason can you think of for remembering those names?

_____

_____

_____

Are any of the names especially appropriate for the characters in the stories? If so, which ones?

_____

_____

_____

_____

Do You Have a Title?

Composing Themes for Titles

About the Lesson

The purpose of this lesson is to make students more aware of the advantages of a good title for stories, essays, and reports. Students in intermediate grades generally write a number of reports, and they may also write quite a few fictional pieces. If your students complete the lessons in this ideabook, they will have many opportunities to practice their titling skills. A good time to administer "Do You Have a Title?", then, is after they have written for one or two other lessons.

Targeted Learner Outcomes

The student will:

- devise titles for eight productions,
- select two of the titles, and
- compose titles for eight works.

1 Open with a discussion of the importance of a good title to a creative work. Many inferior books or movies have benefited from excellent titles. Have students do the exercise. Mention that writing titles, just like any other kind of writing, is a skill that improves with practice.

2 Here students are asked to consider the titles they composed and then choose which two are best. It is important in any creative endeavor that a student learn to evaluate his or her own performance. You can assist your students by helping them develop criteria that are appropriate for good titles. The most effective way to accomplish this is by having a group discussion of what makes some titles effective and others not. Ask:

- Is the title interesting in and of itself? Is it intriguing? Somewhat puzzling? Catchy?

- Is the title sufficiently brief?

- Does the title accurately convey what is to come? (Conversely, is it misleading?)

- Are the words used in the title meaningful to the intended audience?

The final question in this part of the lesson asks students to reflect about excellent titles. Remind them of the criteria you've just discussed. Accept all answers with good reasons.

❸ The final part of the lesson involves the student in composing themes for titles of a short story, a movie, two works of nonfiction, a novel, and a song. Here are brief descriptions of the six titles:

1. Juvenile Nonfiction—*Championship*: National Football League championship games, recounted by Jerry Izenberg

2. Poem—"The Highwayman": the famous ballad about a robber by Alfred Noyes

3. Adult Nonfiction—*Windows to Space*: telescopic and radio astronomy by James Pickering

4. Novel—*The Circular Staircase*: murder mystery, by Mary Roberts Rinehart

5. Short Story—"The Sunday Menace": Robert Benchley's humorous piece about boring Sunday afternoons

6. Song—"Old Shep": song about a dog

The activity concludes the lesson because it gives examples of titles that have been used by successful authors. Your students' guesses about the six titles don't have to be correct, but their ideas could certainly lead to plots for stories, poems, and pieces of nonfiction. Whether you encourage them to write will depend, of course, upon the thinking that they generate in this activity.

Do You Have a Title?

Name _____   Date _____

1 Stories and poems need names so that we can refer to them and tell them apart. In this lesson you are asked to give titles to books, poems, moving pictures, television programs, and short stories that might be written in the future. Write the best title you can think of for each item below. Remember that a good title is usually brief, it arouses the reader's interest, and it gives an idea of what is to come.

What would be a good title for:

1. a short story about a woman whose clothes are the envy of every woman who sees her but whose husband selects all of her clothes because she is colorblind?

   _____

2. a nonfiction book about all of the kinds of nests built by North American birds?

   _____

3. a poem about the contrast between life today and life during
   the days of the pioneers? _____

4. a short story about a dentist who becomes the champion deep-water fisherman
   of the world? _____

5. a motion picture about a race across an Australian desert by two
   men on a camel and two women in a sailboat on wheels?

   _____

6. a humorous poem about a cat that develops the habit of chasing cars?

   _____

7. a movie about an inventor whose failures become successes when his
   daughter shows him how they can be used for other purposes?

   _____

8. a television series in which four boys attempt to open up a business
   selling reconditioned athletic equipment?

   _____

Name _____ Date _____

2 Which two of the titles you wrote in activity 1 are the best for getting someone to read or view the productions? _____

_____

What are the three best titles of books, movies, or TV series that you've heard of?

1. _____

2. _____

3. _____

3 Sometimes a book's title tells us exactly what it is about, as in the case of Ernest Thompson Seton's *Wild Animals I Have Known*. At other times the title is more clever than clear, as in *The Money Moon* and *The Young Man on the Flying Trapeze*. A work of fiction often has a clever, catchy, or enigmatic title, and a work of nonfiction is likely to announce just what it is offering the reader.

What do you suppose these titles are for? Tell what each might be about.

1. Juvenile Nonfiction—*Championship* _____

_____

2. Poem—"The Highwayman" _____

_____

3. Adult Nonfiction—*Windows to Space* _____

_____

4. Novel—*The Circular Staircase* _____

_____

5. Short Story—"The Sunday Menace" _____

_____

6. Song—"Old Shep" _____

_____

Lesson 24

Success and Failure
Writing an Essay

About the Lesson

In today's society students are bombarded with messages telling them that "winning is everything," from the classroom to the athletic field. Implicit in this message is that there is only one winner in any contest. In this lesson, students will explore how they measure success and failure in themselves and in others. Then they will write an essay on this complex topic.

Targeted Learner Outcomes

The student will:

- think about how he or she defines personal success,
- describe feelings about a measure of success,
- learn the essential elements of an essay, and
- write an essay.

1 Open the lesson by asking students to think about what makes them feel successful. When they make an attempt at something—in class, in sports, in band, or even in their relationships with family or friends—how do they know they've been successful? Have students volunteer some of these "measures of success."

Have students turn to the first part of their lesson page, which lists fourteen items. Have them think about how someone would know he or she had been successful in each situation. Ask them to write a "measure of success" for each item. When students are done writing, hold a class discussion about the exercise, listing students' responses on the board.

Now that they've defined success, ask them to define failure. Is failure simply the opposite of success? For example, if fifteen people run a race, when one wins, have the others failed? If any students answer yes to this question, ask for their reasoning and open it up for discussion. (Remind students to be respectful in responding.)

Last, ask students to consider whether people need to experience failure before they know how success feels. Allow students time to discuss the phrase "winning is everything" before moving on to the next part of the lesson.

2 Next, students will write down their feelings about the "measures of success" they wrote in the first part of the lesson. Which is most meaningful to them? Once you've had them thinking about success *and* failure, they may find that their ideas have shifted a bit.

3 Last, after so much discussion and thought about measuring success and failure, students will be ready to write an essay. They can write about one of the scenarios in the first part of the lesson and expand on it, or they may choose another scenario. Here are a few additional choices:

- Winning an election

- Getting your name in the *Guinness Book of World Records*

- Losing 25 pounds

- Finishing a marathon

- Baking the best cake at the county fair

- Being voted the most popular girl or boy in school

- Having a winning ticket for the Irish Sweepstakes

- Celebrating a fiftieth wedding anniversary

- Purchasing a Hummer

If appropriate, students can publish their essays in a student newspaper or class newsletter.

Success and Failure

Name _____   Date _____

❶ How do you know you've been successful at something you've tried to do? Think about the following events. What would have to happen before you would know you'd been successful at one of these endeavors?

1. In business? _____

_____

2. Writing prose and poetry? _____

_____

3. Promoting peace around the world? _____

_____

4. Engineering automobiles? _____

_____

5. Getting good grades in school? _____

_____

6. Being very attractive? _____

_____

7. Playing the piano? _____

_____

8. Cooking? _____

_____

9. Being strong? _____

_____

Name _____ Date _____

10. Recording a song? _____

_____

11. Performing an act of heroism? _____

_____

12. Being a good parent? _____

_____

13. Acting in a situation comedy? _____

_____

14. Being a good citizen? _____

_____

2 Which of the measures in activity 1 is most meaningful to you?

_____

Why? _____

_____

_____

Which measure is least meaningful? _____

Why? _____

_____

_____

Name _____   **Date** _____

❸ How do you define success and failure for yourself? On the lines below, jot down ideas that you can include in an essay about your definition of success and failure. Organize the ideas into an outline.

_____

_____

_____

_____

_____

_____

_____

Before you begin writing the essay, it is a good idea to review these basics:

- The essay is written about one subject.

- It is written from the writer's point of view.

- Arguments are supported with facts.

- The most important points are made at the beginning and at the end.

When you are ready, write your essay on a separate sheet of paper. If you are comfortable doing so, share your essay with the class.

Lesson 25

Trapping
Writing an Essay

About the Lesson

Many young people are not used to "playing around" with concepts, so it takes a while for them to get used to the idea that they are free to let their imaginations take over. They need to become so comfortable that they don't worry about getting correct answers or embarrassing themselves. The enjoyment that comes from using their own ideas will overcome students' fears and defenses. They learn that it is satisfying to think for themselves. In this lesson students will do some of this conceptual thinking, ending the lesson by writing an essay based on some of their thoughts.

Targeted Learner Outcomes

The student will:
- examine the concept of "trapping," and
- write an essay about a trap.

1 Open the lesson with a brief description of the concept of trapping. Ask students for examples of traps. Accept all reasonable answers.

Next, have students complete the first activity, which asks them to think about what kinds of traps would be needed to "capture" the items on the list. As they work their way down the list, the things to be trapped become less concrete and more abstract. Do not require students to fill in every blank. Some of your students may not be able to think of appropriate traps, but there will be others who will astonish you by their perceptiveness.

2 After students have thought of a number of traps, they are asked to devote more thought to one that particularly interests them.

3 After giving the concept of trapping discussion and thought, students are asked to write an essay. In case they are stuck for a topic, suggest these additional items: trapping people into situations in which they are guilty of a crime (entrapping), trapping someone into making a confession or betraying himself or herself, and trapping a person in a romantic relationship.

Before your students write their essays, be sure to remind them that they are essentially making an argument. To be persuasive, they need to arrange their ideas logically and back them up with facts, examples, and anecdotes. They should end with a strong summary statement. Have them give their rough drafts to students they respect for a reading that will show up any flaws in their arguments.

Trapping

 ACTIVITY

Name _____ **Date** _____

1 Have you ever been trapped? People get trapped in floods, in burning buildings, by snowstorms, in quicksand, and in various other ways. Animals get trapped in landslides, in forest fires, and by trappers. When you think about it, there are many other things in the world that get trapped besides people and animals. For example, water gets trapped in sponges and rain barrels. See if you can think of some natural—and unnatural—traps for the following items:

1. flies _____

2. syrup _____

3. music _____

4. heat _____

5. sunshine _____

6. smoke _____

7. laughter _____

8. time _____

9. emptiness _____

10. ideas _____

From *Time to Write*, Copyright © Good Year Books. This page may be reproduced for classroom use only by the actual purchaser of the book. www.goodyearbooks.com.

ACTIVITY

Name _____   Date _____

2 Which of the above items would you most like to capture or to have captured for you? _____

If you do manage to trap it, how long will it remain the way you want it to be?

_____

Why? _____

_____

_____

3 On a separate sheet of paper, write an essay about some kind of trap. Select a situation or process that particularly appeals to you or disturbs you. Jot down your reflections before writing your first draft. (In that way, you'll be able to trap your ideas as they occur to you.)

Before writing your essay:

- Ask yourself whether the topic is really important to you. If it is not, you won't be able to persuade your readers that your essay is worth reading.

- If you are making an argument for or against something, be sure that you have enough facts to back up your ideas and that you have given sound reasons for your point of view.

- Beware of making sweeping generalizations. Try to be specific. Above all, avoid exaggerating.

- The organization of an essay is especially important. Arrange your ideas in a logical manner, placing the strongest points at the beginning and closing sections of the essay.

- Use examples to give the reader a clear understanding of the points you are making and to make the essay lively.

Lesson 26
More Than Enough
Writing an Essay

About the Lesson

There is hardly a time when the media isn't reporting on the scarcity of a natural resource, such as electricity, fuel oil, water, and clean air. It is important that your students be ready to deal with the very serious problems that are brought up in this lesson, including the uncomfortable topic of hoarding.

Targeted Learner Outcomes

The student will:

- investigate the concept of hoarding,
- consider the hoarding that is taking place now,
- contemplate the hoarding that might be taking place in ten years, and
- write an essay about the effects of hoarding.

1 Begin the lesson with a discussion of the concepts of scarcity and conservation or about recent articles on the depletion of the world's supply of pure water or fossil fuel. Then ask students if they would hoard, or acquire more than they need, of any of ten items listed that people have hoarded and are still hoarding. It may seem ridiculous to a student who lives near a lake for anyone to hoard water, but there are many people in arid regions who desperately want to store as much water as they can. Similarly, most young people aren't interested in storing a lot of salt, but a large percentage of the world's population is concerned about having enough salt in the future.

Yet the word *hoard* generally connotes an activity that is dishonorable, disagreeable, and/or sinful. Perhaps a student's attitude about a particular case of hoarding will be determined by the reasons for the hoarding. If the individual, company, or nation hoards because of avarice or ambition, the student is not so likely to feel good about the activity. If the person, corporation, or country hoards in order to survive, the student is more likely to look with favor at the hoarding. Recognizing the sociopsychological reasons for hoarding any of the ten things will contribute to students' understanding of why people behave as they do.

2 If the student hasn't confronted it in the initiating activity, the second level forces him or her to examine the notion that hoarding is justifiable in certain situations.

3 Students are asked to think about the effects of hoarding and write a formal essay about their feelings and ideas. Depending upon how successful your students are at writing effective essays, you might want to give them this checklist when they have finished their first drafts:

1. Did I start with a thesis statement?

2. Do I have facts, examples, and/or anecdotes to support my opinion? (The evidence presented is the most important part of the essay.)

3. Did I avoid the use of broad generalizations or present generalizations that rest upon vague assumptions?

4. Did I organize my facts, examples, and anecdotes in such ways as to make a persuasive argument?

5. Did I demonstrate that I had a clear idea of what I wanted to say?

6. Did I restate my argument at the end of the essay?

ACTIVITY

Name _____   **Date** _____

1   If you could have more than you will need for the next year, which of the following resources would you store up or save?

1. Water? _____ Why or why not? _____
   _____

2. Firewood? _____ Why or why not? _____
   _____

3. Salt? _____ Why or why not? _____
   _____

4. Sugar? _____ Why or why not? _____
   _____

5. Toilet paper? _____ Why or why not? _____
   _____

6. Chewing gum? _____ Why or why not? _____
   _____

7. Soap? _____ Why or why not? _____
   _____

8. Coffee? _____ Why or why not? _____
   _____

9. Flour? _____ Why or why not? _____
   _____

10. Canned fruit? _____ Why or why not? _____
    _____

Name _____   Date _____

People have saved all of these things from time to time. Storing more of something than could possibly be used in the near future is called *hoarding*. Crows, squirrels, and pack rats are some of the better-known hoarders of the animal kingdom. During times of famine, pestilence, and war, people are liable to hoard food or oil or anything that is in short supply.

It is understandable for people to want to get more than their normal needs require. During World War II people tried to obtain as much as possible of items such as nylons, sugar, butter, and gasoline, which were mostly going to the armed forces. Those items were rationed by the government. Each citizen was entitled to buy a limited amount of these items, based upon his or her needs. Generally speaking, the system worked well. In recent time nations have hoarded oil, gold, grain, and nuclear missiles.

2 Are you justified in hoarding anything right now? If so, what?

_____

Why are you justified in hoarding it? _____

_____

_____

_____

3 Of all the effects of hoarding that you are aware of, what bothers you the most? On another piece of paper, write an essay about it. An essay is essentially an argument, and it offers evidence to support the writer's position.

Lesson 27

Winning by Losing

Writing an Anecdote

About the Lesson

This lesson gives students an opportunity to explore the meanings behind the concept of paradox and the meanings of some paradoxical expressions. At the end of the lesson, students will write an anecdote about a paradox.

Targeted Learner Outcomes

The student will:

- learn what a paradox is,
- explain how ten paradoxes can make sense, and
- tell how a personal paradox has had a bearing on his or her life.

1 To introduce this lesson, you might initiate a discussion about paradoxes. Next, talk about the specific kind of paradox in this lesson, such as helping that hinders; it happens a lot at home unintentionally, but it can also be a form of sabotage. And they are also familiar with hindering that helps, as when one person delays another for the purpose of keeping him or her from getting to a surprise party before the celebrants are ready, or when one individual deters another from doing something that shouldn't be done.

2 Then have students do some thinking about the lesson's paradoxes. These are some plausible interpretations of the paradoxical expressions:

1. **Hurting in order to heal:** Often in physical therapy a patient must undergo pain in order to make the body right again.

2. **Healing in order to hurt:** Theoretically, soldiers who are injured in battle are healed by doctors in hospitals so that they can resume their fighting.

3. **Hurrying in order to take it easy:** A great many people hurry through tasks in order to take it easy when the tasks are accomplished, especially if the tasks are disagreeable.

4. **Taking it easy in order to hurry:** They may not do it deliberately, but procrastinators are good at this—by putting things off they put themselves in the position of having to hurry to do what they should have done!

From *Time to Write*, Copyright © Good Year Books. This page may be reproduced for classroom use only by the actual purchaser of the book. www.goodyearbooks.com.

5. **Tightening up in order to relax:** In a situation that calls for tightening up the budget and reducing expenditures, a person can subsequently relax because his or her finances are in better shape.

6. **Relaxing in order to tighten up:** It is often disastrous to push oneself continuously. By letting up a little for a while, a person can then drive forward once again without breaking down.

7. **Flattering in order to belittle:** A person can insincerely flatter another person in front of others so as to puff up that person, and then make fun of him or her later when that person isn't present.

8. **Belittling in order to flatter:** You can belittle yourself so as to puff up another person and thus flatter that person because you have made yourself small.

9. **Spending in order to save:** This is the theme of probably half of all ads, as illogical as it seems. The ads tell the customer that the more they spend, the bigger the savings—but they'll actually be spending more!

10. **Helping in order to hinder:** This paradox suggests the kind of sabotage that occurs in war, but it also is a nasty tactic of people who are intent on destroying a group's goals even though they are members of the group.

❸ Although your students must imagine situations to fit the paradoxes, students' writing will be largely anecdotal. Do not place any restrictions or unnecessary requirements on the writing, except that students should write in paragraphs.

Winning by Losing

Name _____ Date _____

1 Now and then, a wily young person decides to give in to a parent's wishes on a particular issue. The young person reasons that if he or she agrees to whatever the parent wants, perhaps the parent will give in on some other issue later. This strategy is called "winning by losing," which is an example of a paradox.

As odd as it may seem, there have been many occasions when people have found that by losing they could win. Can you think of a situation in which a person could *lose by winning*? Describe it.

_____

_____

_____

_____

2 Here are some more paradoxes. Explain how each one can make sense.

1. Hurting in order to heal: _____

_____

_____

2. Healing in order to hurt: _____

_____

_____

3. Hurrying in order to take it easy: _____

_____

_____

4. Taking it easy in order to hurry: _____

_____

_____

From *Time to Write*, Copyright © Good Year Books. This page may be reproduced for classroom use only by the actual purchaser of the book. www.goodyearbooks.com.

Name _____   Date _____

5. Tightening up in order to relax: _____

_____

_____

6. Relaxing in order to tighten up: _____

_____

_____

7. Flattering in order to belittle: _____

_____

_____

8. Belittling in order to flatter: _____

_____

_____

9. Spending in order to save: _____

_____

_____

10. Helping in order to hinder: _____

_____

_____

3 Choose one of the paradoxes above—or any other one—and tell how it could have, or has had, a bearing on your life. Use a separate sheet of paper.

Lesson 28

Does It Make Sense?

Writing an Anecdote

About the Lesson

"Does It Make Sense?" includes ten statements that can initiate a fruitful discussion—and therefore some thinking. In addition, the statements may prompt students to do further research on a topic that interests them. The emphasis here, though, is on logical thinking.

Targeted Learner Outcomes

The student will:

- determine the reasonableness of ten statements,
- write a logical thinking exercise, and
- write an anecdote.

1 The first part of the lesson resembles a quiz that engages students in analyzing statements. They are to determine the reasonableness of ten statements, each of which might be debatable. By analyzing the statements, students can get a feeling about how tricky language is— much of what we say and write can be misunderstood.

Here are our responses to the question of whether the ten statements make sense. Your students may disagree, but if they do be sure that their reasoning is sound.

1. **Sensible.** We must value beauty. It is one of the characteristics that makes us human.

2. **Sensible.** This is a logical statement inasmuch as it includes the entire universe of objects.

3. **Sensible.** One of the most famous scientific discoveries was that of penicillin. Alexander Fleming discovered penicillin in London in 1928. He found a mold growing on a culture of some common germs, but around the mold that had accidentally grown in a culture plate, he found that the germs were dissolving. Fleming grew the mold on broth and then put drops of the broth in test tubes that contained some bacteria that cause disease. He found that the broth stopped the growth of the bacteria.

4. **Sensible.** Yes, insects, by definition, are animals with three pairs of legs and wings.

5. **Sensible.** Although the husbands of Jerry's two sisters are his brothers-in-law, Jerry's wife may also have a brother, and he is Jerry's brother-in-law too.

 92 Lesson 28: **Does It Make Sense?**

6. **Unreasonable.** It doesn't follow that proficient readers are necessarily skilled mathematicians.

7. **Unreasonable.** If Ned is a vegetarian, he doesn't eat beef or lamb.

8. **Sensible.** Too often shining headlights cause drivers of oncoming cars to run off the road.

9. **Unreasonable.** Mrs. Berry is a native of Louisville. A person is a native of the place in which he or she was born.

10. **Sensible.** Margaret's bare head, especially if she were light-complexioned, could have reflected the sun's rays. However, the yellow field of wheat might have mitigated the effect.

2 Have students create their own logical thinking exercises and submit them to their classmates. In doing so, they will discover that they have to think clearly and consider all of the ramifications of their statements.

3 After giving some guidelines about writing an anecdote, ask students to write one about someone who has acted illogically. There should be plenty of times in which a student has noticed someone acting in an illogical or unreasonable way, but if one or more students become stymied you can cite some examples from comic strips, television programs, or literature to get them started.

Does It Make Sense?

Name _____   Date _____

1 Place an **S** to the left of the following statements that you believe to be sensible. Place a **U** to the left of those statements that you think are unreasonable. Make sure that you understand the terms of each sentence.

_____   1. If something is beautiful, it is also valuable.

_____   2. An object either has color or it has no color.

_____   3. Important discoveries in science are sometimes made accidentally.

_____   4. A six-legged animal with wings may be an insect.

_____   5. All in all, Jerry has two sisters and three brothers-in-law.

_____   6. If Norman is a proficient reader, he is also a skilled mathematician.

_____   7. Being a strict vegetarian, Ned prefers lamb to beef at mealtime.

_____   8. The headlights of the oncoming car blinded the driver of the first car, causing him to run off the road.

_____   9. Born in Louisville, Mrs. Berry is now a native of Baltimore.

_____   10. Margaret's bare head was like a beacon in the yellow field of wheat, reflecting the rays of an unrelenting sun.

ACTIVITY

Name _____   Date _____

2 Why don't you try your hand at writing an exercise like this one? Just
think of several sentences that are logical and some others that have an
element of contradiction or implausibility. Mix them together, and then
try to stump your friends. You can write your exercise in the space below.

_____

_____

_____

_____

_____

_____

3 Write an anecdote about someone you know who acted illogically and
what happened as a result. An anecdote is a short, entertaining account of
a happening, usually personal or autobiographical. It can be one or two
pages long. Your anecdote should be a little story in itself, with enough
details for the reader to get a clear picture of the scene, the characters, and
the action. Anecdotes generally follow a time sequence, and so you can
structure your writing in a chronological manner, thus showing the reader
how things got started, what happened, and how it ended.

_____

_____

_____

_____

_____

_____

_____

_____

_____

Malaprops
Recognizing Malaprops

About the Lesson

In this lesson, students will explore the pitfalls of using malaprops in their writing. Although malaprops are amusing, they can also be embarrassing to the speaker or writer. Because many words can be confused with others that are similar in sound, malaprops are never going to disappear from our speech or writing. At the end of this lesson, students will write about a topic requiring research. The challenge for students will be to use precise language and avoid malaprops.

Targeted Learner Outcomes

The student will:

- recognize the dangers of malaprops,
- write two paragraphs about a topic, and
- do research to back up ideas expressed in the two paragraphs.

❶ Open with a discussion of malaprops. Define this type of diction mistake for students and emphasize the importance of word choice and clarity in writing. Then have students begin the exercise. These are the malaprops in the ten sentences at the beginning of the lesson:

1. *emulated* for *emanated*
2. *granite* for *granted*
3. *indented* for *indentured*
4. *wood-investing* for *wood-infesting*
5. *self-discriminating* for *self-incriminating*
6. *polygon* for *paragon*
7. *anecdote* for *antidote*
8. *aversions* for *aspersions*
9. *derricks* for *derelicts*
10. *sediment* for *sentiment*
11. *skeptical* for *spectacle*
12. *pretty* for *petty*

❷ *Profound* is a good word for a lesson because it is so commonly misused. It means "deep, insightful."

❸ The last section of this lesson explores diction. Students are to write two paragraphs about a topic, making sure that the words they use are precise and correct.

Malaprops

Name _____ Date _____

❶ Occasionally words creep into our speech and writing that seem right when they are spoken or written but are not what we want to say. The incorrect word has the sound or look of the word we want, but it is way off the mark. For example, a newspaper reported that Civil War General Robert E. Lee could not run for president today because he had abdicated the overthrow of the U.S. Government. The article meant that General Lee *advocated* the overthrow of the government, of course. A store advertised a "French prevential bed" not too long ago. This kind of mistake is called a malaprop, after a character in Richard Sheridan's play *The Rivals*, Mrs. Malaprop, who made these gaffes regularly.

Which word doesn't belong in each of the following sentences? Cross it out and write the correct word above or below it.

1. He reported that the rumor emulated from city hall.

2. "That rock is precious," the stonemason asserted. "You shouldn't take marble for granite."

3. "There were many indented servants in those days," the lecturer commented.

4. "The whole structure collapsed because of those wood-investing insects," maintained Mr. Anderson.

5. "I would like to cite my client's protection under the Constitution that he can't give self-discriminating testimony," declared the lawyer.

6. Sheila is a polygon of virtue.

7. "Does anyone know the anecdote for acid poisoning?" asked the distraught mother.

Name _____   Date _____

8. "I won't stand for her casting aversions upon your character!" Mrs. Sabatini said heatedly to her husband.

9. "I wish the city would do something about the derricks and panhandlers," complained Melody.

10. "Her letter was okay in a way, but it lacked genuine sediment," said Lucy.

11. "Ernie was awful," declared Amanda. "He made a skeptical of himself."

12. "That wasn't a serious crime," Jerry said. "It's what they call pretty theft."

Choosing words when you are speaking or writing is called *diction* or word choice. Good diction means choosing the words you need in order to get your meaning across. Faulty diction occurs when you are unsure of what words to use, or when you carelessly use words that sound or look like the words you should be using. The sentences above are mostly examples of the careless choice of words.

2 Some words are commonly misused, as in the case of *profound*. What does *profound* mean? _____

Is that the meaning you have been giving it? _____

3 Write two paragraphs about one of the topics below on a separate sheet of paper. Using your knowledge and without referring to anything or anybody, write at least three sentences for your first paragraph about that topic. Then rewrite your paragraph after referring to authorities or materials that will help you choose the exact words needed to convey your message.

1. The advantages of dandelions over daisies as a food source

2. The breath problem: flossing or gargling—which is best?

3. Plagiarizing of little-known writers when writing term papers

4. The joys of wearing old clothes

5. The strategy of telling the truth in difficult circumstances

Lesson 30
Six for Seven
Imagining Consequences

About the Lesson

In our society the calendar affects nearly every facet of our lives. What would happen if the calendar suddenly changed and every week had six days, not seven? This lesson asks students to imagine how different their lives would be if we eliminated one day of the week from the calendar.

Targeted Learner Outcomes

The student will:

- use creative and critical thinking to imagine and list the wide-reaching consequences of a six-day week, and
- depict one of those consequences in a drawing.

1 The beginning of the lesson poses several questions about changes in our lives if we had a six-day week. In small groups or individually, ask students to think of the changes in everyday life if we were move to a six-day week. (For example, would the number of months in a year change?) It could make a big difference in:

- The work week (Would there still be the forty-hour work week?)
- The consumption of natural resources, such as oil and electricity
- Vacations (Would we still celebrate most holidays on Mondays?)
- Religious services
- Schedules for airlines, buses, and trains
- Cleanliness and sanitation in the city
- The income of publishers of weekly newspapers and magazines
- The sale of sporting goods, including golf equipment
- Attendance at theaters
- The operation of schools
- The consumption of electricity

Allow students time to explore the changes that might take place in their intellectual, social, recreational, economic, and religious lives.

2 The drawing activity at the end of the unit provides a change of pace in having the student draw any scene brought about by the six-day week. Post students' drawings in the classroom.

Following Through

Once students have explored a six-day week, follow up by allowing them time to research how the original seven-day week was determined when calendars were first developed.

TOURO COLLEGE LIBRARY

Six For Seven

ACTIVITY

Name _____ Date _____

1 Imagine that one day you woke up and your calendar had only six days in a week, not seven. In your world, which day has been eliminated?

_____

Why? _____

_____

Let's say that the day that is eliminated is Sunday. Would kids protest because they had only one day off from school? _____

What changes do you see happening if there were only six days in a week? List them here.

_____

_____

_____

_____

_____

2 Take one of your consequences of having a six-day week and draw a scene of what would be happening in your life that would be different than it is now.

The Locked Locker

Writing a Nonfiction Narrative

About the Lesson

This lesson presents students with directions for writing a nonfiction narrative and with an example of one. The sample narrative is a true story of an emotional situation in the life of a middle schooler. The lesson ends with students writing a nonfiction narrative.

Targeted Learner Outcomes

The student will:

- learn the elements and steps for writing a nonfiction narrative, and
- write a nonfiction narrative.

1 Start the lesson with a definition of a nonfiction narrative along with instructions for writing one. Go over the steps in class to be certain students understand each.

2 The tale of the woes of a boy (and his mother) in trying to solve an embarrassing problem with his locker is presented in chronological order. You might mention that some works in this genre incorporate flashbacks and are not strictly chronological.

3 After getting so much instruction about writing a nonfiction narrative, students can begin writing the first drafts without referring too much to the directions for writing the narrative. Then, when they have finished their first drafts, they can go back and look at the directions and the example.

You might also review the elements of a narrative at that time:

Purpose: The primary purpose of a narrative is to recreate an experience so vividly that the reader shares it. You may also want to make a point about people, institutions, or an abstract idea such as fate or luck.

Theme or Story: What is the overall theme of the narrative?

Audience: Who will be reading your narrative? What are they like?

Events: What are the events or actions and who are the characters that make up your narrative?

Point of View: Choose a voice to convey point of view. The first person and the third person (limited or all-knowing) are commonly used.

Plan: In most cases the plan will be organized chronologically.

Revision: Examine your first draft with a critical eye. Look to see if you've presented the events with continuity. It helps a great deal to have someone read your second draft in an objective way. Consider the trial reader's comments and criticisms in writing a final draft. Ask yourself if you are satisfied with the final draft.

The Locked Locker

Name _____   **Date** _____

1 A nonfiction narrative describes a series of events. Some events can be omitted, and some events may get a fuller treatment than others. The essential purpose of the narrative is to allow the reader to follow the events and get a sense of having gone along on the journey or of having had the experience. Because the narrative is usually written in chronological order, it is easy to plan.

Directions

1. Determine your purpose in writing in narrative. Get a clear notion of why you are doing the narrative and express the idea in one sentence.

2. Determine which voice you will use—*I* or *we*, *you*, or *he/she/they*. Generally the first or third person is used. Once you begin to use one of the voices, stay with it until the end of your narrative.

3. Determine the length of the narrative by making a list of scenes and events.

4. Write a rough draft.

5. Read what you have written. Is it too long? Is it detailed enough to convey what you want to convey? Does it move at a good pace? Is it clear? Is your writing understandable?

6. Correct obvious errors.

7. Rewrite the narrative.

8. Look critically at your second draft. Look for mechanics, consistency, clarity, development, and total effect.

9. Have someone read the second draft.

10. Discuss the trial reader's suggestions and criticisms with him or her.

11. Write your final draft in light of those suggestions and criticisms.

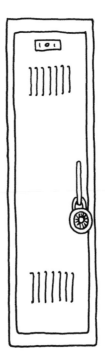

Name _____   Date _____

❷ Following is an example of a narrative, the story of a boy's first days in a new school.

The Locked Locker

Introductory statement/ foreshadowing	This is what happened to a friend of mine—I won't tell his name—when he came to our school last year. My friend almost quit school because of a locker.
First Episode	Before his first day of school, my friend and his mother visited the school. His mother thought it would be a good idea to see what the school was like because they had just moved into town. My friend learned that all students have their own lockers, and he was given the number of his locker and its combination. His mother suggested that they examine the locker because on the first day of the following week he would have to be able to open it. Because he had never opened a locker with a combination lock, my friend was nervous about it. Sure enough, he wasn't able to open the lock. His mother helped him, and they finally were able to open the lock. My friend's weekend thoughts of school were poisoned by fears that he wouldn't be able to open his locker on Monday.
Second Episode	When the dreaded day arrived, he reached his locker a half-hour before the bell was to ring for the first class and struggled with the combination lock for several minutes. When the other students started to crowd around him, opening their lockers, he gave up and went to class. In the first three periods he was given three textbooks and three
Third Episode	assignments. During the noon recess he tried unsuccessfully to open his locker again. Red-faced, he went to the office to make sure he had the correct combination. The assistant principal went with my friend to make certain the lock was operating all right. It was. He put his
Fourth Episode	books into the locker and went to lunch. After the noon hour ended, however, he couldn't open the locker. He went home feeling awful.
Fifth Episode	After telling his mother that he couldn't open the locker, my friend went to his room, but he couldn't do his homework because his books were in the locker at school. When his teachers asked for the completed assignments on Tuesday, my friend wasn't able to hand anything in to them. He went home terribly depressed. "Why
Sixth Episode	don't you have another student help you?" asked his mother when she learned of her son's predicament. My friend said he would ask someone. But because he hadn't made any friends at school yet, he knew that he wouldn't.

Name _____   Date _____

Seventh Episode   On Wednesday he was embarrassed when two of his teachers asked their students to read sections from their textbooks and his were still in his locker. He thought about going to the assistant principal again, but he couldn't bring himself to ask for help. The assistant principal hadn't been unfriendly the day before, but he hadn't been particularly kind either. My friend's only thoughts that evening were of never going to school again.

Eighth Episode   When his mother came home from work, she knew immediately that her son hadn't been able to open his locker. The door to his room was closed, and there were no books on the kitchen table. Being an understanding woman, she didn't press him about the problem. After giving it a lot of thought that evening, she came up with a plan. She'd rehearse opening the locker with him at home until the whole operation was second nature to him. She cut out two pieces of cardboard, wrote numbers on the larger piece, and put them together with a pin, making something that would work like a combination

Ninth Episode   lock. After a good deal of her coaxing, my friend consented to practice moving the small piece of cardboard to the numbers on the larger piece, following the sequence of numbers on a now-crumpled piece of paper. She discovered his problem—he was turning it clockwise when he should be turning it counterclockwise, and vice versa.

Final Episode   Now there was only one more thing she could do to help my friend, but it was risky. Nevertheless, at 6:30 A.M. she drove him to school. Except for a back door leading from the main building to the playground, all the doors were locked. The custodian was in the boiler room having a cup of coffee, so he didn't see a lady and a boy sneak into the building from the rear and head for the lockers in the hall. With his mother watching anxiously, my friend opened his lock the first time. Relieved, she went back home to have a second cup of coffee. He took his books and went to the restroom.

Meaning   That guy's lucky to have such a great mom.

3   Think about a series of events that is true and that has happened to you or to someone you know. Jot down the events on a separate sheet of paper and then write a rough draft of the narrative. Make sure that you have presented enough information so that your readers will have no trouble in following your tale.

Lesson 32
Sketching Someone
Writing a Character Sketch

About the Lesson

"Sketching Someone" takes a straight-forward approach to teaching your students how to write a character sketch, offering directions for writing a character sketch, along with one example.

Targeted Learner Outcomes

The student will:
- learn what a character sketch is, and
- write a character sketch.

1 Have students read the eleven suggestions for writing a character sketch. Emphasize that the first is probably the most important, namely, the subject should be someone that the student knows quite well. Discuss with students the various steps to make sure they understand each.

2 The sample sketch is annotated to show how the young writer incorporated the elements mentioned in the lesson in his character sketch. Point out the annotations to students and discuss any questions they have.

3 After students have completed their first drafts, go over the main points about writing a character sketch. The purpose of a character sketch or profile is to allow the reader to feel that he or she has gotten to know the subject of the piece. It is not organized chronologically but should be organized by topics. The character sketch is informal in tone, and it benefits from quotes, humor, and anecdotes. The writer must first imagine what the person is like to know. What does he or she look like? Where does he or she live? Who are the subject's friends?

Sketching Someone

ACTIVITY

Name _____ Date _____

❶ Writing a character sketch is like painting a portrait of someone. The writer's objective is to present the subject in words so that the reader gets a clear idea of the subject. The subject should be interesting and distinctive in some way, either in characteristics or actions. Readers should be told enough so that they feel that they have met the subject and almost know him or her.

Following are steps for writing a character sketch:

1. Select a person to write about. Choose an individual you know well who should be interesting to your readers.

2. List the subject's characteristics and accomplishments. Underline the most important ones for the kind of sketch you want to write. Each person has an enormous number of qualities, facts, and idiosyncrasies. Your careful selection of these details adds up to the portrait you are trying to create.

3. Decide how you want to portray your subject. Do you want to emphasize your subject's personality, appearance, or character? Simply giving an individual's accomplishments usually isn't enough to hold a reader's interest.

4. Keep your audience in mind. Who will read your sketch? Will your audience be sufficiently interested in your subject to keep reading?

5. Write your rough draft. Don't be too concerned with spelling, punctuation, or grammar at this stage. Leave plenty of space between the lines for corrections.

6. Read over your first draft silently and then read it aloud. Make obvious corrections. Put it aside and don't look at it for a few hours or a day.

7. Read your first draft again, putting yourself in the role of a reader. Does it read easily?

Name _____ Date _____

8. Make the corrections and changes that you see should be made. Look for one kind of error or weakness at a time. Here are the main areas in which possible errors or weaknesses might occur:

- Mechanics: Check your sketch for errors in punctuation, spelling, sentence construction, and grammar.

- Consistency: Is there a logical order in terms of time, plan, importance, complexity, or step-by-step unfolding of the sketch?

- Clarity: Have you given enough details so that a reader can picture your subject clearly?

- Development: Are the main parts of the sketch put together logically? Does the material grow as the sketch develops?

- Total Effect: Do you believe your readers will see, feel, and understand what you have written about your subject? If not, add or remove details so that they will.

9. Give the second draft to someone you respect and ask for frank comments.

10. After the trial reader has read your sketch critically, discuss it with him or her. Make sure you understand any criticisms or suggestions.

11. Rewrite your final draft in light of your trial reader's critique.

ACTIVITY

Name _____   Date _____

2 This is an example of a character sketch that incorporates all the elements listed on the previous pages.

Grandpa, My Favorite Relative

Opening statement/facts

Appearance/facts

Personality trait

My favorite relative was a fighter pilot in World War II, and he's only 5'4" tall. But those 64 inches weigh a solid 185 pounds. Even though he is 79, you'd guess he couldn't be more than 65. Maybe he was blond when he was young, but now his hair is silvery white. There's usually a twinkle in his eye and a half-smile on his face. He looks like a good-natured gnome. Grandpa cracks jokes all the time, but sometimes they aren't very funny. That's all right—he tries.

Glimpse of subject

Personality trait/ examples

Personality trait

When I visit my grandparents, Grandpa is usually busy at his workbench in the garage. He can fix almost anything. Once, when I was young, he fixed my train set when Dad couldn't. The other day he was able to fix the muffler on my dad's car. He just works away at whatever he's doing, but when I ask him a question he likes to explain how things work.

Personality traits

Facts

Quote

Grandpa doesn't talk much about his experiences in World War II or about being a high school principal, and he doesn't try to give me advice. He's a great fisherman because he's patient. Maybe that's why he has been married to Grandma for 51 years. During that time she went from being a flaming liberal to a diehard conservative. When someone asked Grandpa why he put up with Grandma's political shenanigans and occasionally bizarre behavior, he said: "Maybe it's because I love her."

Summary statement/ example

Even though he doesn't tell me what to do, I like to talk with Grandpa when I have a problem. He doesn't tell me I goofed or anything. Mostly he just listens. I guess that's why he's my favorite relative and one of my very favorite people.

3 After you have read the character sketch above and noted the eleven steps in writing one, you should be able to write a character sketch that gives your readers a good picture of someone you know. Jot down your ideas on a separate sheet of paper, then write your character sketch.

Lesson 33

Poetic Licenses
Writing a Character Sketch

About the Lesson

Picture this vanity plate on a parked car: "RISKKIT." Does the extra "K" have a special meaning? Did the owner have a *kit* of some kind for "risking it"? In this lesson students will look at the possible meanings of eight vanity license plates and then write a character sketch about one of the car's owners. (To review the steps for writing a character sketch, see page 106–107.)

Targeted Learner Outcomes

The student will:

- guess about the owners of eight vehicles with vanity license plates, and
- write a character sketch about one of the imaginary owners.

❶ Encourage students to talk about some of the vanity plates they've seen. If there are a few that strike you as more thought-provoking than the ones in the lesson, you can substitute them.

❷ Students will do quite a bit of speculating about the owners of the eight vanity plates that are presented. They are to guess about the age, gender, occupation, and dominant personality trait of each of the car owners.

❸ After imagining what the owners of the cars are like, your students are to write a character sketch of one. To help them, we offer some tips about writing the sketch. If any of your students would prefer simply to choose as a subject someone they know very well, let them write about that person.

Poetic Licenses

Name _____ Date _____

❶ Vanity license plates are available in all U.S. states. If you want a license plate that identifies you or delivers a message, a state will issue it to you for a fee. A vanity plate also gives the car owner a plate that is easy to remember. When you spot a vanity license plate, you may wonder if it is giving a hint about the car owner's personality.

❷ If you saw these vanity plates from behind, what would you imagine the owners to be like? Guess the age, gender, occupation, and a personality trait for the owners of these license plates:

Y R N M W A Y — black Hummer

age _____

gender _____

occupation _____

personality trait _____

M Y X S — Porsche Boxster, silver

age _____

gender _____

occupation _____

personality trait _____

ACTIVITY

Name _____   Date _____

B I G O 2 — dark green Chevy Trailblazer SUV

age _____

gender _____

occupation _____

personality trait _____

G O 2 2 — bright red Honda Accord CRX

age _____

gender _____

occupation _____

personality trait _____

J Z Y 3 — white Toyota Camry

age _____

gender _____

occupation _____

personality trait _____

1 4 A L L — silver Honda Odyssey van

age _____

gender _____

occupation _____

personality trait _____

Name _____   Date _____

S E W M U P — red Ford station wagon

age _____

gender _____

occupation _____

personality trait _____

P D Q 1 — blue Chrysler convertible

age _____

gender _____

occupation _____

personality trait _____

3 Pick one of the owners from the exercise above and think some more
about his or her personality. Jot down your thoughts below, and then on a
separate piece of paper write a character sketch of that imaginary person.
In order to write an interesting character sketch, you'll have to imagine a
number of facts about how the subject looks, how he or she acts, whether
the subject has a family, what kinds of friends he or she has, what the
subject's likes and dislikes are, and what the subject's ambitions are (or,
perhaps the absence of any ambitions).

_____

_____

_____

_____

_____

_____

Lesson 34

Victory for the Victim

Writing a Short Short Story

About the Lesson

In "Victory for the Victim" students will consider how a victim can turn the tables on an oppressor. Working out such a scenario requires some thinking and plot-making. It's a sure bet that students will find one of the activity's situations interesting enough to expand it into a short short story.

Targeted Learner Outcomes

The student will:

- think about and construct scenarios by which victims can emerge victorious, and

- write a short short story based on one of those scenarios.

1 The first part of the lesson introduces the idea that sometimes bullies and others don't profit from oppressing others. Hold a short discussion asking students if they know any examples. There are many, many reports of fraud these days, especially telephone and computer fraud, and so students should be familiar with this kind of crime. To get your students further involved in thinking about people who try to oppress others getting the worst of it, have them write about a possible scenario.

2 Three dishonest people are the subjects of imagined situations in which the tables are turned.

3 In reviewing students' stories you might comment positively when you find elements of the following:

- Verbs of action
- Humor
- Original plot
- Clarity
- Picturesqueness
- Vividness

- Conversational tone
- Naturalness
- Use of quotations
- Logical organization
- Original solution or ending
- Variety in sentence length or structure

Following Through

Students can publish their stories in student publications. For those students who like to sketch, they can draw the crucial scenes of their stories in pencil, crayon, pastels, or other media.

Name _____ Date _____

1   We hear of people being victimized all of the time. In addition to people looking to steal other people's identities, employers are routinely robbed and cheated by their employees, and the general public is often fooled by a hoax or cover-up. It seems as if all of us have to be constantly on our guard.

What if the apparent victim in some cases actually gets the better of the "bad guy"? For example, if a bully hits a smaller boy in the face but gashes his knuckle on a tooth, which then causes a bad infection, he is the "victim of the victim" because he suffers far more than the smaller boy.

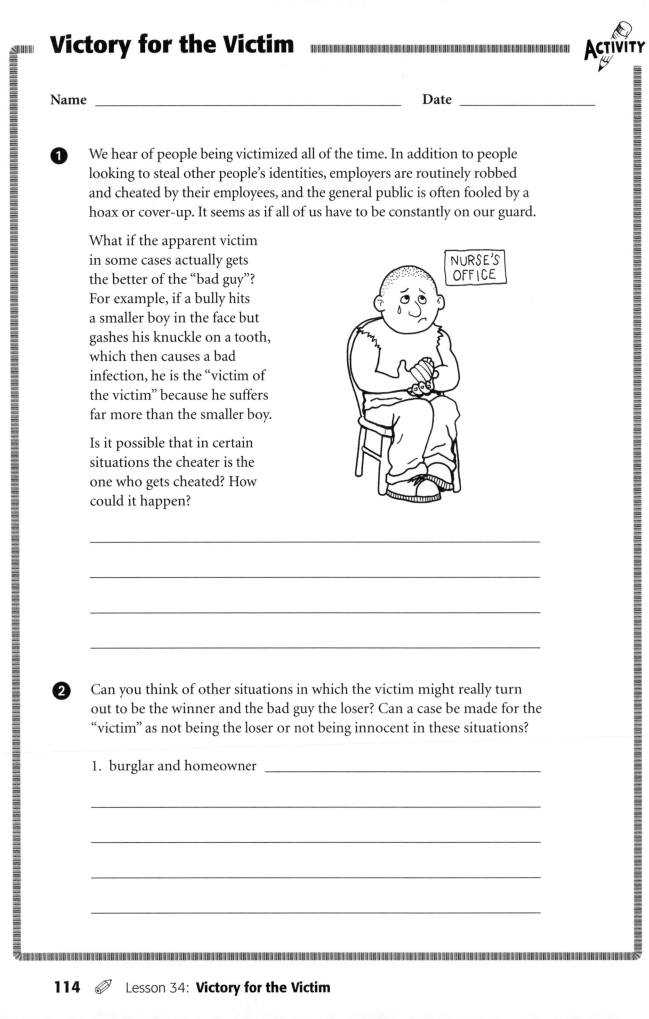

Is it possible that in certain situations the cheater is the one who gets cheated? How could it happen?

_____

_____

_____

_____

2   Can you think of other situations in which the victim might really turn out to be the winner and the bad guy the loser? Can a case be made for the "victim" as not being the loser or not being innocent in these situations?

1. burglar and homeowner _____

_____

_____

_____

_____

Name _____   Date _____

2. real estate swindler and buyer of useless property _____

_____

_____

_____

_____

3. dishonest mechanic and car owner _____

_____

_____

_____

_____

3 Because you have thought about how the victim can turn the tables on the person or persons who has tried to victimize him or her in the situations given above, you have also constructed little plots. Pick one of those situations and expand it into a short short story. You already know your characters, and you have probably placed the characters and action in a setting. All you have to do is give more details and add more color to your plot and you'll have an interesting story.

Sketch out your story on paper or on the computer, and then have a classmate read it to see if it moves along swiftly enough and has enough details to make it understandable and plausible. Then write a second draft with those comments to guide you.

Links

Writing a Short Story

About the Lesson

"Links" is about cause and effect. Some of the linkages are obvious as is the case with the pair of a car accident and a power outage. Others are less apparent, as is the case with a soft drink bottle and a forest fire. What would a soft drink bottle have to do with a forest fire? Maybe your students can think of a suitable scenario.

Targeted Learner Outcomes

The student will:

- think about the links between six pairs of things, and
- select one of those links as the basis for a short story.

❶ Open the lesson by discussing cause and effect. Suggest a few examples. In addition to the example of the wet sponge on the student page, talk about getting sunburned on a day of sunshine and clear sky, eating too many apples and having a stomach ache, or any other experience to which students can relate.

Then have students answer the questions in the first part of the lesson. To find direct or indirect associations between the two items in each prompt, students must create a little scenario in their minds, thus preparing them for writing of short story at the end of the lesson.

❷ One of the six pairs should give students the germ of an idea for a short story. The activity demands that the students think of characters, settings, and actions before responding to each of the six links. In that way, the student can write a beginning for a story that is his or her own.

ACTIVITY

Name _____ Date _____

1 Have you ever placed a dry sponge in a bucket of water? What happens? It swells up. This is an example of cause and effect. The water caused the sponge to swell; the swelling is the effect. There is a clear link between the first event and the second.

Look at the following pairs. In each case, write what you think connects the two items in each pair.

1. indigestion and Daylight Savings Time: _____

_____

_____

_____

2. a car accident and a power outage: _____

_____

_____

_____

3. eye strain and greed: _____

_____

_____

_____

Name _____   Date _____

   4. a soft drink bottle and a forest fire: _____

   _____

   _____

   _____

   5. a dog collar and laryngitis: _____

   _____

   _____

   _____

   6. fear and spring planting: _____

   _____

   _____

   _____

❷   Select one of the connections above that particularly appeals to you and write a short story about it. Before you begin, think about the actors in the story and their personality traits, physical characteristics, and relationships with the other characters in your story. Be sure to give your story a good title, one that will grab the reader's interest. Sketch out your ideas in the space below. Then, on a separate piece of paper, write your story.

   _____

   _____

   _____

   _____

   _____

Lesson 36

What's the Rest of It?

Writing a Story

About the Lesson

Teachers have known for years that one of the best ways to motivate a student to write enthusiastically is to have him or her put something of himself or herself in the work. In this lesson students create an original drawing from some seemingly random lines. Then they develop descriptions about what they've drawn, and, finally, organize the ideas into stories about their creations.

Targeted Learner Outcomes

The student will:

- think about and complete an incomplete figure,
- discuss the drawing, and
- write a story with the drawing as its inspiration.

1 The drawing task should loosen your students' imaginations and free them from some of the inhibiting factors that often stand in the way of creative writing. The lines are not part of the outline of any particular shape, but students will probably find enough stimulation in them to be able to produce some interesting drawings.

Below the drawing, students can create a word picture of what they drew. They can give their drawing all kinds of abilities and attributes. The sky's the limit!

2 After your students have elaborated on the incomplete figure and jotted down their thoughts about what they have done, we ask a series of questions about the drawing, they can write about what feature they like best on their creature.

3 It is not important that the object which the student has drawn be featured prominently in the story; it serves simply as a taking-off point in the student's thinking. It is a good policy to stimulate young writers to think about their story ideas before they begin writing.

Following Through

The most powerful tool a teacher possesses is praise. Find something excellent in each student's story, and tell them. Students will be much more likely to become skillful writers if they hear praise.

ACTIVITY

Name _____   Date _____

1 Look at the lines above. What do they make you think of? Draw a sketch of what you see, using as many of the lines as you like. Add as many lines or colors as you wish.

Use the space below to jot down ideas about your drawing. If you have created an original animal or plant, describe it. If you have drawn a machine, explain how it works.

_____

_____

_____

_____

_____

_____

_____

_____

Name _____ Date _____

2 What quality or ability do you like best about what you have drawn? Does it have one feature that is particularly pleasing or useful?

_____

_____

_____

_____

_____

_____

If it didn't possess this valuable characteristic, would there be fewer or more of these things? Why or why not?

_____

_____

_____

_____

_____

_____

_____

_____

3 On a separate sheet of paper, write a story about what you have drawn. It can be the main focus of the story but there should also be a description of other characters and the setting. Put some action in your story as well. It should move along fairly briskly so that your readers don't lose interest.

Fortunate Misfortunes
Writing a Short Story

About the Lesson

"Fortunate Misfortunes" starts with an activity about blessings in disguise and ends with students writing a short story. It includes a checklist for students to review both before and during the writing of the short story. Students can share finished stories with the class.

Targeted Learner Outcomes

The student will:

- think about and explain how happenings can be blessings in disguise,
- learn what makes a story worthwhile, and
- write a short story.

❶ Have students read the definition and example of the term "blessing in disguise." Mention any of your own experiences that qualify as blessings in disguise and ask students to share their own stories.

❷ Have students write their thoughts on the twelve situations in this section of the lesson. How could each event change into a blessing in disguise? Following are suggested responses:

1. A fire in the kitchen could result in the discovery of faulty wiring in the building and thus the building could be made safer.

2. Cutting your thumb could mean that you use the other hand and find that you are better with that hand for certain things.

3. If you get lost in a strange neighborhood, you might learn of good places you were unaware of, or you might meet an accommodating person to help you find your way and thereby acquire a friend.

4. Losing a game often becomes a blessing in disguise because it is a "wake-up call" concerning your overconfidence or the need to improve a particular skill.

5. Forgetting someone's name could result in your taking a course in how to remember names, faces, and other important information, thus enabling you ever after to be a whiz at remembering names and faces.

6. If you drop your sandwich in the dirt, someone might give you part of hers or his, starting a friendship.

7. Losing a purse or a wallet might convince you that you should be more careful, changing your habits when it comes to carrying valuables in the future.

8. Not making the soccer team could give you more free time for studying, and that might result in raising your grades.

9. Forgetting a loved one's birthday is bad, but it might provoke you into giving the person a present you might not have given that is very appropriate and is highly appreciated.

10. Confusing one person for another could mean that your eyesight is defective, thus convincing you that you should get an eye examination.

11. Choking on a chicken bone could possibly result in someone's making you cough it up with the Heimlich's maneuver, thus giving you an incentive to learn that and other resuscitation techniques that will permit you to rescue others.

12. Falling down could be an indication of a problem with your inner ear, which might bring to light a medical problem that can be improved or cured.

3 In planning their short stories, your students should use one of their own responses for the kernel idea of the plot. Have them glance at the checklist provided in the activity and then write their rough drafts. They should look at the checklist more carefully after they have written that first draft, but no one should worry too much if he or she doesn't have all of the elements on the checklist.

Fortunate Misfortunes

Name _____   Date _____

❶ A blessing in disguise is an event or situation that seems to be very
    unfortunate for an individual, but subsequent events turn it into a
    blessing. For example, a famous movie star was a promising dancer as
    a teenager, but an injury to her leg ended that career, forcing her to try
    singing instead. Her singing with a big-name band launched a glittering
    career in films.

❷ Following are some happenings that at first seems to be the result of very
    bad luck. Try to think of how each can turn out to be a good thing. How
    can the happening be a blessing in disguise?

    1. A fire in a kitchen: _____

    _____

    _____

    2. Cutting your thumb: _____

    _____

    _____

    3. Getting lost in a strange neighborhood: _____

    _____

    _____

    4. Losing a game: _____

    _____

    _____

    5. Forgetting someone's name: _____

    _____

    _____

ACTIVITY

Name _____ Date _____

6. Dropping your only sandwich in the dirt: _____

_____

_____

7. Losing a purse or wallet: _____

_____

_____

8. Not making the soccer team: _____

_____

_____

9. Forgetting a loved one's birthday: _____

_____

_____

10. Confusing one person for another: _____

_____

_____

11. Choking on a chicken bone: _____

_____

_____

12. Falling down: _____

_____

_____

ACTIVITY

Name _____ Date _____

3 You undoubtedly have some good ideas about what might make the above events into blessings in disguise. Choose one of the events that interests you. On the lines below, write an outline for a story about how that event becomes a blessing.

_____

_____

_____

_____

_____

Now you're ready to write a short story based on your outline. Before you begin writing, take a look at the following checklist of things that will make your story strong:

A good story should have:

1. An interesting subject

2. An interesting title

3. A plot that builds up to a climax

4. Humor

5. Expressive and imaginative words

6. A sufficient amount of action

7. Enough detail

8. The element of surprise or suspense

9. The effect of arousing the reader's emotions

10. Complete and well-constructed sentences

11. Proper punctuation

After reading the checklist, write your rough draft on a separate sheet of paper. When you've finished the draft, look at the checklist more carefully. Do these apply to your story? Make any changes and write your final draft.

Lesson 38
Surprise Letters
Writing a Short Story

About the Lesson

"Surprise Letters" begins with a true tale of an amusing incident. The story presents students with a mystery to solve and a springboard for writing their own stories.

Targeted Learner Outcomes

The student will:

- solve a mystery,
- recall a humorous mix-up, and
- write a story featuring a mix-up.

1 Ask students to read the story about Mike, Bill, and the case of the painted mailbox. Explain to students that they should give this mystery some thought. Why did Mike not see anything different about his mailbox when he returned home from his weekend trip? Ask students to come up with at least one plausible explanation.

2 Next, students should write about how they would deal with this dilemma if they were Mike or Bill. There *is* definitely a problem because someone has the wrong name on his or her mailbox. What should Mike do? What should Bill do?

3 Next, have students think about any mix-ups they or someone they know have experienced. Then ask them to write about that mix-up in a story.

Surprise Letters

Name _____   **Date** _____

1 Mike, an electrician in his mid-twenties, had just moved to a new home near the beach, and he wanted to make sure that local postal carrier knew where to deliver his mail. One day he mentioned to his friend, Bill, that he was planning to paint his name on the mailbox at the end of the one-block street on which he lived. His was one of three mailboxes at the end of his street. Mike said he would probably do the job in the next week.

On Saturday, Mike left town to visit some friends. This gave Bill an idea. Because he especially enjoyed doing lettering and decorative artwork, Bill thought he would go over the next day and letter his friend's name on his mailbox as a surprise gift.

The following Monday, the two men ran into each other outside and talked about the weekend. Although Bill waited expectantly, Mike never said a word about any decorations on his mailbox. On Tuesday, Bill asked Mike how he liked the lettering on his mailbox. Mike was astonished to learn what Bill had done, for when he had collected his mail that day and the day before, he hadn't seen anything different about his mailbox.

Can you explain why Mike did not see his name on the outside of his mailbox?

_____

_____

_____

_____

_____

From *Time to Write*, Copyright © Good Year Books. This page may be reproduced for classroom use only by the actual purchaser of the book. www.goodyearbooks.com.

ACTIVITY

Name _____ Date _____

2 At first the two young men were baffled—why hadn't Mike seen the artwork on his mailbox? Then, together, they realized that Bill must have painted the wrong box! They both roared when they thought of the surprise that someone must have had when that person went to get the mail on Monday.

What would you have done if you had come to your mailbox one day and found someone else's name elaborately painted on it?

_____

_____

_____

_____

What would you do next if you were Mike?

_____

_____

_____

_____

If you were Bill, what would you do next?

_____

_____

_____

_____

3 Do you know any other stories of humorous mix-ups? On a separate sheet of paper, write a short story about that mix-up.

Let's Change the World!
Writing a Play or Story

About the Lesson

This lesson asks students to do a kind of thinking called "transforming." there are ten transformations to think about, and some of them are challenging ("What would you make stretch so that it would be more successful?"). The exercise concerning making the world better leads to the question of how the student's life would be changed if one of the transformations took place, and that leads in turn to an invitation to write a skit or play about someone with superhuman powers.

Targeted Learner Outcomes

The student will

- explore ways to make the world better,
- describe how life would be if one of those changes happened, and
- write a play about someone with superhuman powers.

1 Open the lesson by asking students to think about one thing they would change about the world if they could. Allow some discussion and then tell them that they are about to spend some time imagining some specific changes. Give students enough time to finish the exercise. Then, again, ask for discussion. Some students may have trouble with some of the items, so a class discussion may help those students think more creatively about the items. Remember, there are no right answers.

2 Have students choose one item from the first part of the lesson and write a paragraph about that change. Explain that they should include details about how the change would affect their own life. After students are done writing, hold a class discussion about students' responses.

3 Movies about superheroes like Spiderman and Batman have been very popular in recent years. Here is a chance for students to imagine what life would be like if they were superheroes themselves. In the lines provided, have students jot down an outline of characteristics and powers they'd have. Ask them to think about their plot—how would they use their powers? Then, on a separate sheet of paper, have students write a short play based on the outline they've written. The play should have at least two characters whose dialogue moves the action. After students are done writing, have them pair up and practice each other's plays before presenting them to the class.

Following Through

"Let's Change the World!" adapts itself particularly well to science and social studies units. Here is an excellent opportunity for your students to examine humans' relationship to the environment. How much of his environment can people change? The serious part of this exercise is that students will be stretching their thinking and seeing consequences that have personal and societal implications.

Let's Change the World!

ACTIVITY

Name _____ Date _____

1 Sometimes, when things aren't going too well for us, we'd like to change the world to suit us. In this exercise you'll be given an opportunity to imagine that you can change things to the way you'd like them. If you had the power to do so, what things would you change?

1. What would you make lighter so it would be healthier?

_____

2. What would you make quicker so that it would be less painful?

_____

3. What would you make odorless so that it would be more appealing?

_____

4. What would you make shorter so that it would be easier?

_____

5. What would you make clean so that it would be more comfortable?

_____

6. What would you make stretch so that it would be more successful?

_____

7. What would you make straight so that it would be simple?

_____

8. What would you make natural so that it would be more attractive?

_____

9. What would you make green so that it would be funnier?

_____

10. What would you make faster so that it would be more economical?

_____

ACTIVITY

Name _____ Date _____

2 Describe how life would be if any one of the things you have named above were changed as suggested. How would this change *your* life?

_____

_____

_____

_____

_____

_____

_____

_____

_____

3 Make up a skit or a play that features someone with superhuman powers. You can use the space below for outlining the plot or writing part of the dialogue. Then write your play on a separate sheet of paper.

_____

_____

_____

_____

_____

_____

_____

_____

_____

_____

Lesson 40
Warnings for the Unwary
Writing a Humorous Speech

About the Lesson

There are people who are very good speaking to groups extemporaneously, but the great majority of us have to write out a speech before giving it. That gives us a chance to organize our thoughts, to find weaknesses, to add and subtract portions that need strengthening, and so on. We try to give your students a taste of this kind of writing with "Warnings for the Unwary."

Targeted Learner Outcomes

The student will:

- examine a dozen pieces of dubious advice,
- invent some humorous warnings,
- learn about writing a humorous speech, and
- write a humorous speech.

1 The lesson starts off with a dozen pieces of advice that most people would find rather silly. Ask students to read the list and answer the questions. Guide students to see the humor in these dubious bits of advice.

2 The next level asks students to compose their own silly warnings. Give students time to think up some creative bits of advice.

3 After choosing one of the warnings, students are to write a humorous speech. You can follow through with this part of the lesson by having your students actually deliver their speeches. It's not easy to write humor, and some of your students may struggle with this assignment, so don't insist that all of your students deliver their speeches. Nevertheless, each of your students will learn something by attempting to write a humorous talk.

Warnings for the Unwary

ACTIVITY

Name _____ Date _____

① Here are a dozen random pieces of advice. Read each one carefully.

1. Never pour syrup with your left hand if you are right-handed.

2. Don't pick up pennies in revolving doors.

3. Always wear rubber-soled shoes while repairing electric toasters.

4. Be careful in your dealings with people whose eyeglasses fog up all of the time.

5. Don't entertain friends right after your little brother has been watching "Spiderman."

6. Keep your mouth closed if you ride a motorcycle.

7. Listen carefully to people who don't look you in the eye when they speak to you.

8. Watch out for cats that swish their tails—you may be the prey.

9. Don't use dollar bills for bookmarks.

10. It's a good idea to wear shoes if you dance in the kitchen.

11. Always wear gloves when you grab an eel.

12. Don't ask your best friend whether you are wearing the right clothes.

Which of these pieces of advice
do you find most useful?

_____

_____

_____

_____

ACTIVITY

Name _____ Date _____

Which would you be least likely to follow? _____

_____

Why? _____

_____

_____

_____

❷ Some of the above warnings are fairly silly. Can you think of humorous warnings you'd like to share with others? Write them here.

_____

_____

_____

_____

❸ Think about one of the warnings in this lesson and use it to write a humorous speech on a separate sheet of paper. On the lines below, jot down your ideas of what you'd like to say in the speech. You can use understatement, exaggeration, puns, irony, satire, repetition, and/or slang to amuse your audience. (Don't overdo exaggeration or repetition, though.) In addition, when you deliver your speech, you can use emphasis, long pauses, facial expressions, variations in speed and volume, eye contact, and other devices to get across the humor.

_____

_____

_____

_____

Lesson 41

A Mixed Blessing

Writing a Research Report

About the Lesson

This lesson starts off with a story about a girl who has a problem. The story leads into an exercise that involves explaining how a number of fortunate happenings can become mixed blessings. Students are then to extend their thinking to consider a variety of predictions for society that can have favorable and unfavorable consequences. The idea of the lesson is to interest students in one of the future developments and have them do some research concerning it.

Targeted Learner Outcomes

The student will

- understand what a mixed blessing is,
- learn the guidelines for research, and
- write a research report about predicted developments in our society.

1 Preview the lesson's story for students: Tiffany wants very much to get a part in a class play, lands it, and then finds out that she is expected to make her own costume. The mixed blessing derives from the fact that she doesn't have the money with which to buy the materials. Students must find a solution to Tiffany's problem.

2 Next, your students are asked to explain how eight situations could be construed as mixed blessings. For the most part, students won't have any difficulty explaining why the situations have both positive and negative implications.

3 Finally, students must consider some predictions of things that could happen in the future and then do some research about one of them. At the end of the lesson, students will find tips for doing research. This activity, then, is not one that can be done in one or two class periods. In requires some research and writing out of class. Students can do the first two parts of the lesson in one class period and they can write the research report over a period of several days.

A Mixed Blessing

Name _____   Date _____

1 More than anything, Tiffany wanted to be in the class play. At the try-outs, Ms. Morris, her teacher, recognized that Tiffany could handle one of the larger parts. Tiffany was overjoyed when one afternoon Ms. Morris posted the list of cast members. She and several of her friends had won roles in the play. They'd start rehearsing the next day.

At that first rehearsal, Ms. Morris passed out scripts and made an important announcement. "Because we don't have any money for our play," she said, "we'll be making the props, and each person will be responsible for providing his or her own costume."

Tiffany's heart sank. Her father had just been laid off his job, and only two days ago he'd told his three children that they wouldn't be getting allowances until he found work. She knew that her part required a fancy costume. Tiffany and her mother would be able to sew the costume, but they had no material in the house with which to make it. She had foolishly spent all of her savings on a new DVD last month and was utterly broke.

Tiffany's good luck in landing the prize part in the play was completely offset by her despair at not having the money to buy the material for her costume. What could she do?

2 You have probably had a few experiences similar to Tiffany's, when an apparent good stroke of luck brought with it some elements that weren't so fortunate. Examine the following situations and tell how they could also be mixed blessings.

1. Being given a dog with a pedigree: _____

_____

_____

Name _____ Date _____

2. Being an excellent piano player: _____

_____

_____

3. Being extremely beautiful: _____

_____

_____

4. Being extraordinarily handsome: _____

_____

_____

5. Winning $500,000 in a lottery: _____

_____

_____

6. Striking oil accidentally in your backyard: _____

_____

_____

7. Being awarded a scholarship by a nearby college: _____

_____

_____

8. Being the only one in the group with a driver's license: _____

_____

_____

Name _____   Date _____

❸ There will be many developments in the future that will change the way we live. Some will seem like a boon—but, upon further reflection, they may turn out to be mixed blessings. A number of people, for example, think television is a mixed blessing. Take a good look at the predictions for the future that are listed below. Then choose one, circle it in the list, and then tell what you think the advantages and disadvantages of it might be.

Predictions

- A 20-hour work week

- Automated assembly lines for cars, trucks, and other vehicles

- Twice as many people living on Earth during the next century

- The warming of Earth because of the increasing amounts of carbon dioxide in the atmosphere

- Rapid depletion of oil reserves

- Europe becomes one country with one government.

Advantages

_____

_____

_____

_____

_____

_____

ACTIVITY

Name _____ Date _____

Disadvantages

_____

_____

_____

_____

_____

_____

_____

Now that you have given some thought to what might be the advantages and disadvantages of the development, look into it more thoroughly. Research the subject. Then, with the information you will gather about the predicted development, write a research report of your findings. Following are guidelines for doing research.

Guidelines for Doing Research

1. **Read.** Read carefully. Take notes on points that you think are particularly important.

2. **Think.** Don't believe *everything* you read. Just because something is in print doesn't mean it is correct. Examine what you read with a critical eye.

3. **Check.** If what you read seems hard to believe,
    a. compare it with other sources of information,
    b. decide how reliable the material is by learning more about the author or editors,
    c. examine the date of publication (How recently was this published?), and
    d. determine how well supported the material is.

4. **Understand.** Try to get an overall idea of your material. Find someone, such as a teacher, parent, or librarian, who can help you to interpret difficult passages.

Finish the Story

Writing a Story and Drawing

About the Lesson

Story starters are good for students who have difficulty deciding upon a theme or plot when asked to write a story. Most students, with a little prodding, can decide upon a beginning for their stories, but many need help developing the rest of the story. This lesson is designed for those students who need a little assistance in getting their stories launched.

Targeted Learner Outcome

The student will

• write a story inspired by a story starter.

1 In this lesson students will get the chance to develop a story from a story starter. First, have them read the nine story starters provided, answering the questions that follow each. This lesson requires some time for creative thinking, so you may want to spend a few days on just the story starters.

2 There is space provided for students who want to sketch a scene from a particular story. This will help them write a complete story later.

3 After students finish answering the questions, ask them to choose the one that interests them most to develop into a complete story. Students who are more visual should feel free to illustrate their stories.

Following Through

You can celebrate student stories in any number of ways: with a mural on a class bulletin board, a bound class book, or even with skits or oral readings. Give each student a chance to present his or her story to the class.

Finish the Story

Name _____   Date _____

1. It was seven o'clock in the morning. There was no one on the beach.
   More logs and kelp were on the beach than had been there the day before.
   Nancy stopped and turned toward the sea. She stood still for a long time,
   looking out at the water.

   What did Nancy see?   _____

   Why do you think so?   _____

   _____

   Draw what she saw.

   What happened next?   _____

   _____

2. Jan turned the corner. She looked up at the tall building next to her.
   Then she stopped. She tilted her head back and stared. Three people
   also stopped near Jan and looked up.

   What did Jan and the three people see?   _____

   What makes you think so?   _____

   _____

   Draw what Jan saw.

   What happened next?   _____

   _____

Name _____ Date _____

3. Henry squinted. He placed his hands at right-angles to his brows
   to reduce the glare. Then he began running very hard over the
   snow-covered slope.

   What did Henry see? _____

   Why do you think so? _____

   _____

   Draw what Henry saw.

   What happened next? _____

   _____

4. Larry was coming to the top of the hill. He walked past a big tree. Two
   birds were singing noisily. Then he looked to his right. He saw something
   dark in the ground. It was a big hole. Something darted into the hole.
   Larry went over to the big hole and looked in.

   What did Larry see? _____

   Why do you think so? _____

   _____

   Draw what Larry saw.

   What happened next? _____

   _____

Name _____ Date _____

5. Henry leaned back in his chair. He closed his eyes. Then he tapped his foot on the floor. Slowly, he began to move his lips.

What was Henry doing? _____

What did he hear? _____

What will he do if someone comes into the room? _____

_____

Tell the rest of the story. _____

_____

_____

6. Frank lifted his lead from the pillow. Then he arose from his bed and went slowly to the window. He opened the window a little and listened. Then he closed the window and went back to bed. He lay still, but then he lifted his head once more and listened.

What did Frank hear? _____

Describe the sounds. _____

What happened next? _____

_____

7. Lisa ran across the room, snapped off the television set, and then ran out of the room sobbing. The elderly man seated in front of the set slowly turned his head as she fled the room. He fingered the broad red and white suspenders that held up his spotless work pants and then lowered his chin on his chest.

Why was Lisa disturbed? _____

How old is she? _____

Who is the old man? _____

Is he related to Lisa? _____

Name _____   Date _____

Where did the scene take place? _____

When did it take place? _____

What happened next? _____

_____

8. Although Evelyn pulled hard on the leash, Molly dug her feet into the ground and wouldn't budge an inch. It started to rain harder, and Evelyn began to get angry. She shouted at the big Labrador to move, all the while jerking on the leash. The dog began to growl.

Why wouldn't Molly move even though Evelyn pulled on her leash?

_____

Where might Evelyn and her dog have been? _____

How old do you think Evelyn is? _____

How old is Molly? _____

What is she like? _____

What happened next? _____

_____

9. The musicians were enthusiastically playing the last chorus of a rollicking tune when suddenly one of the trumpeters put down his horn and scrambled off the bandstand. He grabbed one of the dancers by the arm and let out a cry of joy.

Why did the trumpet player rush down among the dancers and grasp one of them by the arm? _____

Why was the musician so happy? _____

What kind of dance hall were they in? _____

What kind of person was the trumpeter? _____

What happened next? _____

_____

Lesson 43
Questions about Your Future
Writing a Personal Letter

About the Lesson

This lesson invites students to look seriously at their futures. Five questions, taken from a high school student's written concerns about her future, lead off the lesson. The students are then asked to compose five more questions concerning their futures. Finally, they are invited to write a letter to themselves with some predictions about what will happen in twenty years.

Targeted Learner Outcomes

The student will:

- answer five questions about his or her future,
- compose five additional questions about the future and answer them, and
- write a letter to himself or herself.

1 Introduce the lesson by talking briefly about the works of George Orwell, Ray Bradbury, Jules Verne, H. G. Wells, or any other science-fiction writer. Now that students are in the mood to imagine the future of the world in general, tell them that in this lesson they will be thinking about their own futures. What will they and their lives be like in twenty years? Ask students to take a look at the first part of the student page. Explain that these are five questions a student wrote about her own future. Have students spend time answering these questions for themselves. If they need more space to write, they can use the back of the page or a separate sheet of paper.

2 Now have students write and answer five more questions about additional topics affecting their future lives. If they are stuck, mention topics such as war, health, companionship, and faith.

3 To prepare students for this part of the lesson, review the form for a friendly letter—a letter to oneself should certainly be friendly. Provide envelopes, if possible. This is an activity that should provoke considerable reflection, so allow as much time as possible.

Following Through

The logical follow-through of the lesson is to get the students together after twenty years and have them read aloud their letters. However, an easier and more immediate follow-through is to have them discuss their overall feelings about the future or to pick out one issue that is common to everyone (e.g., jobs) and lead a discussion about it.

Questions about Your Future

Name _____   Date _____

1 Here are five questions a high school student asked herself. She was quite concerned about her future, and maybe you are too. Can you answer these questions for yourself? Give it a try.

1. Are we running out of everything? Will there be enough oil, food, housing, and money for people for the rest of my life?

_____

_____

_____

_____

2. Do I really want to spend the rest of my life engaged in the career I choose now? Will it be too late to switch later on?

_____

_____

_____

_____

3. What if my parents or guardians died tomorrow—what would I do?

_____

_____

_____

_____

Name _____   Date _____

4. Will there be enough jobs twenty years from now?

_____

_____

_____

_____

5. How do I feel about growing old?

_____

_____

_____

_____

2 Now ask five more questions of yourself about your future. Answer your own questions as well as you can.

1. _____

_____

_____

_____

_____

2. _____

_____

_____

_____

_____

ACTIVITY

Name _____ Date _____

3. _____

_____

_____

_____

_____

4. _____

_____

_____

_____

_____

5. _____

_____

_____

_____

_____

3 Because you've given some thought to ten difficult questions about your future, you can put your thoughts together by writing a letter to yourself. It should contain a few predictions. When you have reviewed the letter and written a final draft, address it to yourself and seal it. Put it in a safe place, to be opened in twenty years. Your letter should prove fascinating reading.

Index

Index

Index

Index